FACEBOOK MARKETING: INTERMEDIATE GUIDE

The Intermediate Guide to Facebook Advertising that Will Teach You How to Increase Your Facebook Ad Conversions, How to Develop Your Skills, and Scale Up

BRYAN BREN

Thank you for downloading this book!

In order to thank you, **I would like to offer you a complementary download** about 5 social media marketing tips you should know before reading this book.

[CLICK HERE TO GET IT AND STAY IN TOUCH](#)

© Copyright 2019 - All rights reserved.

The content contained within this book may not be reproduced, duplicated or transmitted without direct written permission from the author or the publisher.

Under no circumstances will any blame or legal responsibility be held against the publisher, or author, for any damages, reparation, or monetary loss due to the information contained within this book. Either directly or indirectly.

Legal Notice:

This book is copyright protected. This book is only for personal use. You cannot amend, distribute, sell, use, quote or paraphrase any part, or the content within this book, without the consent of the author or publisher.

Disclaimer Notice:

Please note the information contained within this document is for educational and entertainment purposes only. All effort has been executed to present accurate, up to date, and reliable, complete information. No warranties of any kind are declared or implied. Readers acknowledge that the author is not engaging in the rendering of legal, financial, medical or professional advice. The content within this book has been derived from various sources. Please consult a licensed professional before attempting any techniques outlined in this book.

By reading this document, the reader agrees that under no circumstances is the author responsible for any losses, direct or indirect, which are incurred as a result of the use of information contained within this document, including, but not limited to, — errors, omissions, or inaccuracies.

Table of Contents

Introduction: Back in My Day… 7
Chapter 1: Facebook's Past, Present, and Future 14
Chapter 2: Next Level Facebook Advertising 26
   Understanding Facebook's Ad Delivery Algorithm 27
   Pixels and How to Use Them 38
   Targeting the Right Audience 48
   Back to Basics...57
   The Takeaway.. 66
Chapter 3: Modifying Your Medium........................... 68
   The Versatility of Facebook..................................... 72
   Boost Your Posts 77
   Image Ads.. 82
   Video Ads 89
   Mixed Media Ads... 96
   Facebook Ad FAQ..101
   The Takeaway...105
Chapter 4: Facebook Mobile 107
   Facebook's Demographics..................................... 108
Chapter 5: The Marketplace 116
   Advertising Vs Listing 119

The Takeaway 126
Chapter 6: Facebook Jail 128
The Takeaway 135
Chapter 7: Rethinking Your Brand 137
How to be a Better Marketer 144
Conclusion: Beyond Facebook 147
References 149

Introduction: Back in My Day…

Before I say anything else, I must emphasize that the strategies covered in this book are intermediate techniques. A basic understanding of Facebook, marketing and advertising, and business is a prerequisite, so if you're looking for the fundamentals, I recommend that you read my first book in this series, *Facebook Marketing Step-By-Step*. In it, I show you how to set-up, operate, and market your business on Facebook even if you have no knowledge of how to use the platform, or are just starting out in your entrepreneurship. This intermediate guide assumes that you have either read my introduction to Facebook marketing, or already have your foundations in order.

Forgive my shameless plug, but I had to warn you. I won't spend that much time revisiting the basics, and you'll benefit the most from this book if there is no need for such. With that out of the way, let's talk about Facebook, and why taking your advertising there to a whole new level is a step in the right direction.

I'm willing to bet that at some point in your life, you

thought to yourself that Facebook was dying out. With the rise of other social networks—Twitter being its greatest competition—many people assumed that Facebook's time was up. Trends have always dominated how we socialize and interact with each other. Facebook, like everything else, got to a point where it was no longer the cool kid and interest in it began to wane.

I've met quite a few young people who believe that Facebook is an "old people's website". They assume that it's the platform you use to keep in touch with your technologically disadvantaged grandparents, or to seem like a "normal" person to employers without becoming fully corporate as you would on LinkedIn.

You may assume the same right now; that Facebook is no longer the place to be, and is just another account you feel obligated to have as an entrepreneur, on the off chance that you might reel in some Baby Boomers.

This assumption is wholeheartedly wrong.

Recent reports show that Facebook has approximately 2.5 billion active users. By comparison, that's twice as many as YouTube—the giant in social media influencing. Furthermore, on this list, WhatsApp and Instagram rank third and fourth respectively, and guess what? Facebook owns them both. Then you have Reddit at number five, and only then you'll see Twitter with 330 million active users. Facebook's primary competition has been blown so far out of the water, it doesn't even have 20 percent of Facebook's following (Stout, 2019).

Tell me again how Facebook isn't the cool kid? Tell me again how it's dying out? Tell me one more time how it lost its favor to trendier platforms?

Facebook *is* the trend, and that's because its creators set it up to withstand the test of time. It's not to say that other social networks are fleeting, and I am sure they'll stick around for many years to come, but Facebook did what the others didn't: everything.

Facebook was not the first of its kind. Two social networks in particular paved the way for it: Friendster and Myspace. Both failed because they didn't accommodate their users.

In the case of Friendster, it was pretty much what Facebook is today—a place for friends, family and old acquaintances to keep up with each other, share posts with each other, and stay up to date with events and happenings. Its biggest mistake was only catering to one audience. At the height of its success, Friendster decided to change the website into a platform for gamers. Those who wanted to continue using it as a social network were disregarded, the gamers didn't take the bait, and the site met its end shortly after (Horsman, 2016).

Myspace overshadowed it in this time and started out as the giant of the online world. It was in a class of its own. But, its failure was brought about in its attempt to be something it was not—versatile. Myspace began as a network for performers. Musicians could post their music and share tour dates with followers. That was it. It then grew and became a place for everyone to share their lives and that was when it hit its peak. Myspace didn't account for its growing fanbase and when it dawned on those in charge that the website was dominating, greed took over and it was sold to corporate types, who immediately began changing the website's operation to appeal to even more people.

The website didn't do it properly, and ended up driving their existing user base away… right into the arms of Facebook, which didn't have the same bugs, listened to its users and did what Myspace tried to do exceptionally well. In Myspace's attempts to keep up, it lost all of its appeal and had no choice but to copy Facebook to stay in the race. The problem was that Facebook was the better of the two, and no one wanted Myspace anymore, so it died (Lee, 2011).

Facebook set itself up to maintain its user base from the very beginning. It was built to last, and so naturally did. Which is why now, in its 16th year, it's still going strong. Myspace had a good run for five or so years, while Friendster existed for 13 years, but faded long before it officially shut down.

Back to how Facebook does everything. Let's compare it to its current competition. YouTube is a website for video creators. There is a clear divide between observers and creators, and so the platform does what the money asks of it. Instagram (which again is owned by Facebook) is an app for photo-sharing. Sure, you can post short videos there as well, and there are massive marketing opportunities you can wield on it, but people go there to look, not communicate. Twitter is for microblogging. It limits your characters and isn't really designed for photo or video sharing. Its premise is also that you can be anonymous, and that you don't have to connect with the people who pay attention to you. While it's excellent for celebrities, influencers, and others who enjoy chopping down what they have to say, the fact remains that it's lacking in experience for both its users and its visitors. I won't even start on what there is to complain about with the 'new' kids, TikTok and Snapchat.

Facebook, on the other hand, evolved with the times. It never committed to one single thing, and so was able to expand flawlessly when more was expected of it. Do you want to share a video? Post a photo? Have a short rant? What about a long rant? Do you want to have a long rant about the video you have shared? Perhaps you'd rather indulge in a hidden object game? Buy or sell something from the classifieds? Market your rock band from a separate account so that your old aunty can't see you cussing? Or, maybe you just want to use Facebook as it was almost twenty years ago, to find that cousin you lost touch with, or message that long-lost friend you haven't seen in years.

Facebook does all of that, and so it appeals to everyone. In marketing and advertising there is strength in numbers, and Facebook has that perfected. Imagine all the social networks as passengers on a bus. There are no seats left, and Facebook—the old man—gets on. What do the others do? They move out of the way so that Facebook can sit and rest its legs—a privilege it's earned time and time again.

Now that you understand how much of a giant Facebook actually is, you'll have a better idea of how much employing the following strategies can have a positive effect on your business. You're not just marketing, your marketing to the masses. All that you have to do is up your game beyond the fundamentals.

Chapter 1: Facebook's Past, Present, and Future

One of the most important skills you have to develop as an advertiser is some fortune-telling. Forecasting can make or break your business. It's what you use to plan, manage, and operate your resources. Make the wrong decisions and your business will take a knock. Guess correctly (and intelligently), and you'll watch the money pour in like a waterfall. One thing that's overlooked too frequently in advertising and marketing is forecasting not only your business, but the platforms you use to operate your business on too.

It's understandable that you don't put as much thought into it as you should. Social media platforms are trendy. They rise and fall all the time, and word of their popularity (or fading popularity) will spread to you even if you don't research it. If they fail, you'll just pop up on the next cool platform ready to go. Seeing it this way is a rookie mistake, because that's how ordinary users look at it. If Facebook were to vanish tomorrow, those who have no important reason to use it won't really be impacted. Those who rely on Facebook as an income stream will.

Even if you only use a Facebook page for your business, that is an income stream—or at the very least a potential one. If Facebook goes, your customers go with it. While it's inevitable that Facebook will expire someday, your job as a responsible entrepreneur is to see it coming a mile away, to the best of your ability.

So, before we get into the real advertising techniques that you can implement on Facebook, I want you to take a quick look at the platform's climate. This way, you can better determine how and when to use the strategies that will follow, and will have a better understanding of how far into the future they can serve your business.

Then

To gauge where Facebook is headed, you'll have to understand where it comes from. A lot can be said for its progression, adaptability, and growth, and so its future is easier to analyze and predict. So where did it all begin? I've already mentioned that Facebook wasn't the first of its kind and how its competition of the time lost to it, so I won't touch on that again. Instead, I'd like to describe Facebook as it was. If you weren't around for it, you may be surprised by how basic it was.

Facebook began in 2004, when its creator Mark Zuckerberg was a Harvard-based student of psychology. He had engineered other social media platforms just for the fun of it, including a website similar to Tinder, called Facemash—upon which users could rate each other based purely on attractiveness or aesthetic. The Facebook—as it was then called—was nothing more than a network of Harvard student profiles. It caught on immediately and within one day, more than 1,000 students had signed up for it (Phillips, 2017).

Also, in 2004, Facebook's first trace of advertising was implemented. It was called "Flyers", and as you can imagine, it functioned as an online noticeboard. Students (and other small companies) paid to use this feature to market themselves and their products or services. It was Zuckerberg's way of fundraising to support the website.

Within The Facebook's first few months it had grown so popular that it spread to other universities. It then branched out to include high schools, and only two-and-a-half years after its inception became Facebook as we know it, in name and in function. By September 2006, Facebook had dropped the idea of listing academics only and went worldwide, accessible to anyone with an email address and friends they wanted to keep in touch with. By December 2006 Facebook had 12 million users. By October 2007, it had more than 50 million users. You don't need a Ph.D. in business to understand how exponential Facebook's growth was.

In 2007, Facebook launched its Ads platform, where for the first time, users could boost their own content through paid promotion. Facebook Ads gave users insights and aimed to promote content to users who displayed interest in similar content. This paved the way for Facebook's targeted ads in 2009.

Facebook was a social network in the truest sense of the word. It didn't focus on appealing to strangers, being seen, or getting unnecessary attention. It was wholesome, if not a bit oversimplified in its design, but it promoted the sense of online community. This is easily observable when you consider that for most of Facebook's history, there were only two possible reactions to content: liking and sharing. There was no downvoting or disliking anything unless you took the time to explain why in its comments or your own status before sharing something.

Facebook didn't build itself up on the fan-follower model that every other social network used, and that sense of community bred communication—and is where Facebook's true strength lies.

Now

Facebook is unrecognizable to what it was before. It has leaned more towards the commercial, fan-follower dynamic, but only if you want it to be so. It never remodeled its set-up to accommodate popularity over experience, and that could also be a driving factor as to why so many people love it. You don't need millions of followers to make the most of the platform, and those who have two friends get the same features and experience as those who have an entire army of supporters. Everyone is equal on Facebook, it's still free for everyone to use, and it's one of the few platforms that makes its money not by coercing users into buying premium access or paid features, but through advertising. What changed is how we use it.

It evolved from a simple profile listing into the most comprehensive social network that we have. Sure, you can still use Facebook to keep track of your crush and express what you're doing or thinking about, but that's the tip of the iceberg.

Facebook is streamlined to work for any and every body that joins the site. You can share nonsense on it, livestream, buy and sell, promote your art or business, follow your favorite celebrities, join groups of like-minded people; set up, schedule or join events, donate to charities and have fundraisers of your own; you can control who sees your content; you can apply for jobs, message customers (or friends) directly, play games, set up surveys and polls, and post or share any sort of media you can imagine, from links, to videos, to gifs, to photos and by means of your profile, even audio too. Facebook functions as a contact list, portfolio, gallery, office, and entertainment center. If you want to share memes there, go ahead. If you have to do work, switch to your business page and go ahead with that instead.

Some of its features, like setting up a business page or group, are preset for optimization based on what you need it for, so we can say that Facebook can function as your website too. Heck, it's even got audio and video calling enabled through Messenger, so it can be your business center if you need it to.

The difference between Facebook and competing apps, websites, and platforms is that the latter focused on what you use it for (videos on YouTube, microblogging on Twitter and so on), whereas Facebook focuses on the fact that you *do* use it.

More people have a purpose for Facebook than any other social network and that's what sets it apart.

Statistics show that a whopping 93% of social media marketers advertise on Facebook (Andersen, 2019). It's no wonder when you consider Facebook advertising as we know it today. It still allows promoted posts, but its placed ads have become more effective as the design of the website has evolved. Now, marketers have access to a range of analytics and a variety of advertising choices (from placed ads to video marketing) that weren't an option when Facebook first started out.

Advertising as a whole has begun to drive social media, so when you marry Facebook, the biggest social media platform, with advertising, where all the money is, it's a recipe for success. Facebook is one of the very few platforms where ads aren't invasive, and the platform itself can effectively be used for marketing whether you're paying for advertising or not.

As an entrepreneur, you can't overlook how much power Facebook can give you. But as I said, it's bound to expire sometime. When will that be? It's worth it to invest in Facebook advertising *now*, but what will become of your Facebook business in the foreseeable future, and what does that mean for your marketing strategies?

The Future

In May 2019, Facebook was hit by a blackout. Rumors spread that the website was under a hack attack, but the company denied it, explaining the downtimes as a fault on its own part. Changes to their system didn't take well and so the website (and all associated apps including Whatsapp and Instagram) went down (Donie O'Sullivan, CNN Business, 2019). Do you know what happened in that time? People lost their minds. I was one of them, so I speak from experience. Facebook is one of those things that a third of this planet's entire population can't live without. If it goes down, that's 2.5 billion people who are left angry, frustrated and ready to make heads roll.

Based on this alone, Facebook isn't going anywhere anytime soon. From where we're standing, Facebook will be the giant for as long as it has no direct competition. Following this logic, it can only go up and change in ways that will keep it on top. Here are the scenarios that are most likely to occur:

More Profile Features: Users are sure to gain more control and design over their profiles, and hopefully this will bleed into the business side of things as well (since currently business pages are quite uniform and lacking creativity for page owners).

Timeline Changes: Just as the profiles are bound to change, usability has to update too. Facebook has proven its ability to adapt time and time again, so nothing is stopping it from keeping up with advancements in technology, for example by adding functionality for 3D content (which the platform is already implementing) or virtual reality. It's also likely that audio will feature more prominently outside of profiles and Messenger, as users have shown interest for years.

Facebook Will Engineer More Apps: It was reported that 2019 closed off with Facebook dominating app downloads entirely. All four of the most downloaded apps of the decade (Facebook, Messenger, WhatsApp, and Instagram) fall under the company (Perry, 2019). It's logical to assume that as Facebook acquires more business, it will integrate their services into the main app and go on to create or take over other apps that Facebook has no room for. The more apps Facebook acquires, the more people will stay with Facebook as well.

You'll Have More Competition: One problem is that as Facebook grows, so will hostility on it. It's easy to do business when you're one of five people in the spotlight, but if all businesses migrate to Facebook, you become another number that has to fight for scraps of attention. That's why it's important to grow your audience and establish your place now, before your competition catches on. It's quite the double-edged sword. Your audience will grow, but your reach will be more difficult to maintain.

Facebook Might Become More Commercial: This is bound to work in your favor. Facebook has already set up ways to transfer money, it's just that most people are still using other cash transfer services like Paypal, Payoneer, credit cards or even just good old banking. However, with Facebook's fundraising, payments, and MarketPlace options, we can predict that sending money through or over Facebook will be integrated with more sophistication in the future.

Advertising Will Evolve: Compared to other social media platforms, Facebook has resisted blasting sponsored content from influencers onto your timeline. Most ads are placed before or in between the content you are looking at, but it can't avoid forced ads forever. It may be annoying, but this also serves you well. As I said, Facebook is funded by advertising. The more ads that feature on the platform, the more money you can make as a business there.

The Takeaway

Facebook continues dominating online media and social networks and it's unlikely to lose its rank, power, or reach any time soon. It's got the upper hand in advertising because of the sheer number of features it has. It's the definition of mass appeal, and so caters to businesses that need an audience.

Facebook's design and features make it so easy to set efficient marketing strategies for yourself and then follow through. It's also easy to predict where Facebook is headed so that you can plan ahead, give yourself a head start, and set yourself up for success.

Chapter 2: Next Level Facebook Advertising

Regardless of how much power Facebook has, no amount of marketing or advertising on the platform will benefit you if you don't understand how advertising on it works. I've noticed that many entrepreneurs who are new to marketing only do so on a surface level. Sure, you might get a few clicks and the new engagements or customers that it brings will feel amazing, but that's only the tip of the iceberg. Too many entrepreneurs set up their Facebook page or ads and just post a status or two then call it a day.

This elementary approach won't get you very far because you'll only be promoting yourself to the people who are already paying attention to you. It's preaching to the choir.

Beginner marketers tend to research all the strategies, tricks, and cheats to grow an audience, but place emphasis on the wrong aspects of marketing. Being seen is one thing—and it's necessary to effective advertising—but it's not as important as making sure that you're seen by the right people.

Who might that be? The people who want to throw money at your business.

Intermediate marketers have to let go of the "Friends and Family" mindset. Yes, you want your nearest and dearest to support you, and the people who like and care for you are the most likely to share your posts, comment on your stuff, and recommend you to others, but most of the time they're not buying you bread. You are a business person, and it's high time you stopped relying on people who aren't aiding your growth for support.

And so your first intermediate lesson begins with something you're probably heard of, but don't understand as well as you should: algorithms.

Understanding Facebook's Ad Delivery Algorithm

I'm sure that you've heard influencers (or computer geeks) mention "the algorithm" time and time again. YouTubers especially enjoy complaining about the algorithm because the platform keeps changing it and so creators have to alter their content to keep up with it. Why though? What is "the algorithm" and why do influencers change what they do to suit it? Why is it so important to follow it?

To properly explain this, you first have to understand what an algorithm is. In mathematical terms, an algorithm is an unambiguous process, rule set, or list of instructions one has to follow in order to complete a calculation or to solve a problem. That's all it is—the steps you take to get from A to B.

You use algorithms all the time in your daily life. GPS directions, recipes, tutorials, and instruction manuals are all examples of what algorithms are. But we're not talking about daily life, so what do algorithms have to do with your business and advertising?

Well, computers use algorithms too. They're the core of coding (in most programming languages) because computers can't think for themselves the way we can. Everything your computer (or other devices) does is by instruction. I'm no coder, so I won't fill this chapter with math and science, but in layman's terms, algorithms tell your computer exactly what to do based on the input you give it.

Algorithms exist in all facets of computing, including online and on social media platforms.

The most important part that you need to focus on is how they deliver content to users.

How Facebook Reads You

Using YouTube as a simple example, its algorithm prioritizes which content you see first, which plays a massive role in which videos are featured, trending, or viral on the platform. The problem is that the algorithm that chooses these videos changes with the wind. Since these creators make money from their videos, they have no choice but to abide by what the algorithm demands.

On Facebook it's simpler. The algorithm shows you content based on what you like and engage. So, if you like pages, join groups, and share posts to do with cooking, Facebook's algorithm decides that you need more cooking content shown to you. This also applies to the updates you see from friends. The people you have the most in common with, or the people that you interact with the most, will take priority on your feed and you'll see more of them (Mosseri, 2018).

You don't have to think about that though. What you should focus on is that it's that same algorithm that determines which ads are displayed to which users.

But how does the algorithm decide what's good content for users and what should be disregarded? According to Brandwatch, the algorithm calculates the best content viewing content presented to you based on four things: inventory, signals, score and predictions (Boyd, 2019). Signals are by far the most important to marketers, so we'll disregard the other three for now.

Signals, in layman's terms, are the elements to a post—any post—that determine how it's curated and displayed on the website or app depending on its quality. Generally, the following is included:

- Like, comment and share count.
- Interaction and engagement on a post.
- The time at which the post was made.
- Devices used and the specs of digital content.
- The poster's profile, and how detailed it is.
- Information presented in a post (relevance, accuracy or even potentially harmful content).
- The type of content (text, image, video, multimedia etc.).
- Average engagement time.

So, when you are setting up a post for marketing purposes, it's a good idea to check all these boxes so that it scores higher and the algorithm feeds it to more people. Over-optimization won't trick the algorithm into prioritizing your posts or ads if the content you are sharing is low effort, inaccurate, scammy, full of spam, or otherwise empty.

Getting the algorithm to work in your favor is as simple as creating content that it's programmed to promote. The rabbit hole goes a little deeper though, because artificial intelligence is at play too.

Machine Learning and Why It Matters

Machine learning, simply put, is what computers use to make decisions without your input. By comparison, a traditional algorithm has set input for predetermined results. In this context, machine learning is what drives the ads that are displayed to you. If you click like an ad (input), an algorithm will show you more or similar content (output).

Machine learning is far more interesting, because it's a form of artificial intelligence and is therefore programmed to mimic logic rather than order. So, a machine learning algorithm could decide that since you joined a vegan group, you might be interested in a vegan restaurant near you, or an anti-animal cruelty page. By the same token, machine learning would figure out that you won't be interested in a Meaty Monday special, or supporting makeup companies that test on animals.

More mainstream instances of this fascinating technology include navigation apps, email filters, digital assistants like Siri and Alexa, search engines, fraud detection software, video surveillance, and even automated tech support (Daffodil Software, 2017).

There is one problem with Facebook's machine learning algorithm, and that's that it knows more about you than you do. In 2018, the company and Mark Zuckerberg himself came under fire for involvement in a privacy controversy—now called the Facebook-Cambridge Analytica Data Scandal. It came out that Facebook was selling user data without consent to Cambridge Analytica—a political consulting firm that used the data to control reception of political ad campaigns.

During the investigation of the Data Scandal, it was discovered that Facebook knowingly and willingly uses a machine learning algorithm to predict what users will buy to more efficiently advertise products or services (Sam Biddle, 2018). This in and of itself is not a scandal. Machine learning is a logical advancement in our technology and predictions are just one of its many uses. What those on the outside didn't like about the reality of it is that firstly, the document that exposed this was marked as confidential and Facebook users weren't aware of it, and secondly, it can be construed as manipulation.

You'll have to make up your own mind about this one. Is machine learning prediction a great leap forward, or is it brainwashing? Many people argue that it's weird and an invasion of free will to have machines advertise stuff you don't know you need yet.

No matter which side of the fence you fall on, machine learning is a fact in the matter, and one that you'll have to be on board with if you're going to use Facebook as a marketing platform.

The Sales Funnel

Just in case you need a refresher (or are a little bit lost in this intermediate strategy), a sales funnel is a model you base client purchases on. Think of it as your very own algorithm. It details the steps you will set up for your customers to compel them to buy from you. Your sales funnel will be whatever you make it, but it should look a little something like this:

- Awareness
- Interest
- Evaluation
- Decision
- Purchase

By now, you should already have your sales funnel set up and ready to rock, so I won't bother you with the step-by-step or elementary explanations of what each of the mentioned phases are. However, I will assume that what you don't know is that the sales funnel you already have doesn't work on Facebook. You're going to need a new (or at least separate) model to work from, or else you won't see much money on the platform.

See, the standard sales funnel applies to standard business. It works extremely well if you have set up shop in a mall, or run an ecommerce store, or have set up your own spot on an ecommerce websites, like Amazon, eBay, or Etsy. That's because people who are browsing such websites or indeed browsing in a shopping center, already have the intention to spend money. Facebook is not an ecommerce website, so most of the people on it have no intention at all of making purchases when they log on (Zakowski, 2015).

Facebook isn't the first thing to come to mind when you think of online shopping, so it's definitely low on the list of things that come to mind when customers want to spend money. By all definitions it's a social network, so it's not unbelievable that most users log on to… you know… socialize.

Your Facebook sales funnel has to take low buying intention into consideration, or else you might as well advertise to a brick wall or a park bench. In fact, you may have more success marketing to a park bench because it doesn't have the sentience to scroll away from your ads.

Think of traditional advertising. Sure, TV commercials don't appeal to everyone who looks at them, but that's where strategy comes in. Advertising carpet cleaner during prime-time television is a good move because if you have a TV, it's safe to say that you have a home. That home likely has at least one carpet, and that carpet will inevitably need to be cleaned. Play that ad over and over again, throw in a catchy jingle, and the next time you notice that your carpet looks a bit shoddy, you'll be motivated to go out and spend money on the carpet cleaner you saw advertised. A simpler example is advertising car insurance on a billboard seen from motorways.

Ad placement is everything. You wouldn't promote carpet cleaner to the homeless, and you wouldn't market car insurance at a bus stop. If you did those things, sure, maybe one homeless person will remember you when they get out of their fix; and maybe the bus driver will take some notes and call in after their shift, but why would you invest your time, money and energy in advertising to the wrong people?

Entrepreneurs often forget that most people on social media don't care about what they have to offer. It's a harsh reality, and I mean no offence, but just because there is a massive audience in front of you, it doesn't mean that they're your audience. Comedians don't perform in between acts of a ballet, and Britney Spears wouldn't open a show for Slayer. That's not how it works. Not in the real world, and not on Facebook.

So, to maximize buying potential on Facebook you have to understand that most people online aren't interested in what you're advertising, and then create a sales funnel that hits the people who are interested in you right in the face. Here's what it should look like:

- **Awareness:** Phase one doesn't change. You still have to promote yourself to as many people as you can. However, you have to let go of your desire to reach as many people as possible, and opt for targeted advertising instead. In most cases, the algorithm takes care of this for you, you just have to learn to optimize it.

- **Engagement:** Once your ad is placed properly and is reaching the right people, you have to motivate them to click on your ad. Just as any other business will have incentive to pull people in, you have to get people to interact with your ad, business, page or posts on Facebook. Engagement counts because you are paying for your ads, and if no one clicks them it's a waste. There's also potential for ad revenue, which you might only earn per click. Negotiation, research, quotes and otherwise finalizing a purchase all happen through engagement.

- **Conversion:** Once you've got a customer locked in, it's easier to sell to them. Ultimately, what you want is for this conversion to happen from the client's side without any more intervention from you. To achieve this, you're going to need some sort of call to action (CTA) set up. It could lead clients to your mailing list to enable further promotion in the future, you could direct them to your website, or platforms outside of Facebook, and, best-case scenario, you could lead them straight to a purchase—the ideal CTA, especially if you're selling directly on Facebook's platform.

It's easier said than done, but it's the only way to efficiently promote your business on Facebook. If you don't implement phase one—awareness—properly, you won't see engagement, and you won't have any conversions. So, let's focus on how you can go about targeting your ads to the correct audience, to boost your sales.

Pixels and How to Use Them

Chances are high that if you're a beginner marketer, you don't know what pixels are and are missing out on how they can boost your business. To clarify, I'm not talking about pixels in imaging. Marketing pixels are a whole new ball game—one that you're going to learn how to play. You may not have heard of pixels before, but you sure have experienced them.

Have you ever searched for something on the internet, only for ads for that exact thing to show up when you visit unrelated apps or websites? The FBI isn't watching your every move, and you're not having your mind read. Pixels are responsible for the precise ads that are regularly displayed to you.

In marketing, pixels are snippets of code that function as trackers. If you visit a website, open an email, or log into an app that uses tracking pixels, it means that your data—other sites you've browsed, actions you took online, browsing time, and so on— is collected for third parties to view and optimize their ads based on your behaviour.

You can use tracking pixels as a marketer to target your ads more effectively. It's not rocket science, and doing so can truly take your advertising to the next level. But, before I tell you how, I must answer one question that I'm sure you're bursting to ask.

Are Tracking Pixels Legal?

Collecting data from website visitors sounds like it should be a crime. If the thought of having your online habits on display makes you uncomfortable, you're not alone. From a business perspective, using pixels might feel dirty. You can rest easy. You won't go to jail if you use tracking pixels, but it comes with an important caveat.

You can only track user data with consent. This is why you can't visit websites without agreeing to their privacy, cookie, and data collection terms of service. There's a story behind why one day no one cared, and the next we all received an influx of emails from various companies informing us that they were updating their privacy policies.

In 2018, the European Union implemented the General Data Protection Regulation—revisions to standard laws that no longer served the protection of personal information of EU citizens. Though these regulations weren't added to other legislation (as far as I can see), most websites would be affected because of the sheer number of Europeans who use them. So, the GDPR became the norm across the globe, even if only in spirit or as a precaution (Tulie Finley-Moise, 2019).

The GDPR has updated many, many laws and there is way too much to discuss in detail, but in a nutshell the most important changes include:

- Mandatory notifications in the event of data breaches.

- The right for users to access their own data, including the right to know why and how their data is being processed; the right to correct or request deletion of data; and the right to know how long their data will be stored.

- Mandatory prioritization of user data protection and security.

- The right for users to transfer their personal data, including accessing their own data in various formats, and transferring data from one controller to others (both within reason).

- The right to erasure. This is perhaps the most interesting one, as it details that users now have the right to have their data permanently deleted. Note that it depends on circumstance in most cases, and does not apply to all users or instances.

Furthermore, the GDPR implemented seven principles that participating entities must abide by when processing data—including the collecting, storing, transfer, erasure, organization, combining, communication, and rectification of data, among others. These principals are:

- Transparency

- Limitation
- Accuracy
- Confidentiality
- Accountability
- Purpose Limitation
- Necessity

These are in place so that data will be processed safely, lawfully and ethically in order to best protect users and user privacy. It may seem like pixels are the exact opposite of ethical, but there's a loophole that you are more than welcome to exploit: User agreement.

One interesting stat, that may push you even further away from pixels, is that most people don't bother reading the Terms and Conditions that they agree to. In fact, almost all Americans couldn't be bothered, with surveys showing that 90% of adults don't read the privacy policies on websites before consenting to them (Cakebread, 2017).

I know that sounds bad, but this is intermediate marketing. You can't afford to be a softie. To be frank, whether users understand the terms they agree to is not your circus and therefore those are not your monkeys. So long as the user consents to the privacy policy, marketing pixels—within the boundaries set by the GDPR—are perfectly legal and therefore a tool that you can use to make more money.

Facebook Pixels

Now that we've cleared that up, we can get back to business. No two pixels are the same, and Facebook has its own tracking pixel that advertisers can make use of. The Facebook pixel will give you insight to how users behave on your website once they interact with your ads. It will also show you information across platforms and devices, so that you can improve your ad experience for users on desktop, mobile, browsers, the app, or even people who switch between these. New text suggested to add

It's wise to set up your pixels as soon as you can, even if you don't have any ads up on Facebook yet, as the pixels will track data that will aid future advertising. It's not difficult to do, and you'll have given yourself a big head start by thinking ahead.

Facebook allows you to set up pixels for 17 predetermined actions, called Events, in your business manager ("Specifications for Facebook Pixel," n.d.). These events are a list of standard, foreseeable behaviours that users are likely to display, and will tell your pixel what to keep track of. If the predetermined ones aren't what you're looking for, you can also set your own custom pixel. The standard events, which will be tracked on your website, are:

- Add payment info
- Add to cart
- Add to wishlist
- Complete registration
- Contact
- Customize product
- Donate
- Find location (when users search for your company's address)
- Initiate checkout
- Lead (for when a user signs up to a service without payment, for example, joining your mailing list or having a free trial run)
- Purchase
- Schedule

- Search
- Start trial
- Submit application
- Subscribe (for users who sign up and pay for subscription services)
- View content

You can customize these standard events by setting your own parameters for them, though this will require some coding, so for the sake of simplicity, we won't get into that. There's simply too much to cover because of the endless possibilities and variables.

How to Set Up Your Facebook Pixel

You'll have to log in to your ad manager on Facebook to create your own pixels. Once you're in, here's the step-by-step on how to do it.

- **Step 1:** Navigate to your Events Manager.
- **Step 2:** From the menu icon (which will appear as three horizontal bars at the top of your screen) select 'Pixels'.

- **Step 3:** A green "Create a Pixel" button should appear at the bottom, or center of your screen. Click it.

- **Step 4:** Fill in the necessary information—your website's URL and your chosen pixel name—and when you're ready, click 'Create'.

- **Step 5:** Select how you're going to add the pixel to your website. Options include manually adding the code to your site's html, widget integration, or emailing instructions to your developer. If you're using a widget, it will do everything for you and there is no need to move on to the next step. The same applies to sending the code to your developer as they will take it off your hands. However, if neither of those apply, you're going to have to do it yourself.

- **Step 6:** To add your pixel to your site manually, you are going to have to do a bit of coding. Note that if you're not using a template on your website, you're going to have to manually insert this code into every page. Copy the generated code from Facebook, go to your website's code, and paste it between your header tags. This is what I mean: <high-density your Facebook code here</header>

- **Step 7:** Select "Automatic Advanced Matching". This enables your pixel to find Facebook users who have shared their information with you through your website already.

- **Step 8:** Next, you'll have the option to do a test run. All you have to do is insert your website's URL in the search bar and then click "Send Test Traffic". The red dot above the search bar will turn green once the pixel begins tracking. When this occurs, hit 'continue'.

- **Step 9:** Your pixel is set up, so all that's left is some optimization. You'll see a menu that you can use to select the actions (from the list of 17) that you would like to track. Turn on the ones you need and deselect the ones you don't.

- **Step 10:** When your preferences are in order, the pixel will do the rest. All that's left for you to do is to update your own privacy policy on your website. This is so that you'll be compliant with Facebook's policy, and won't get into trouble later.

- **Bonus step:** If you use Google Chrome, you can add the Facebook Pixel Helper extension to your browser. This add-on will show you if your pixel is up and running.

Once you have your pixel set up, what you choose to do with it is, quite literally, your business. You don't have to use pixels if you can't move past tracking the activities of others, but doing so will up your game in targeted advertising. On a platform as broad and as passive as Facebook, this is a trick you can't afford to disregard.

Targeting the Right Audience

Now that you understand that Facebook isn't like the other social networks, you can go about adjusting your advertising so that it reaches the right people. You've probably heard the term "targeted advertising" thrown around, and I have brushed over it, but before we continue, let's clarify what exactly target advertising is.

Basically, it's a method of advertising in which ads are placed according to the demographic, behaviour, or other traits of the viewer. Remember my analogy of car insurance advertised on motorway billboards? That's one example. Another would be placing ads for women's products in groups, pages, and videos that women are likely to frequent. The targeted advertising rabbit hole runs deep, because with the right optimization, you don't even have to guess. Some ads can be set to only display for the ladies, or Europeans, or adults over 40. Targeted ads are shown to you based on the information that you share online, be it your email address, Facebook profile, or (through pixels) actions. Facebook has its own ways on targeting ads to certain audiences, and you, as an advertiser, have a fair amount of control when setting this up.

Before you do that though, you'll have to have a solid understanding of who you want to target so that you can define your best audience or audiences online. You can do a little bit of manual market research if you like, but pixels and analytics will make a world of difference if you don't have the means to survey or observe your audience outside of Facebook.

Once you have figured out who you are catering to, you can start planning your targeted ads. Facebook allows you to target your content to people based on the following:

- **Automatic Optimization:** The simplest way to target your ads is to let Facebook do all the work for you. Its machines will match audience data to your business, product, or service and display its ads to people most likely to take interest. This is a good option if you don't have a specific audience in mind for your business (as you would if you were to market children's toys to parents).

- **Behaviours:** Facebook will use the pixels you have set up to market your ads to the people who have already shown interest in what you do. It's an excellent way to capitalize on your engagements outside of Facebook.

- **Demographics:** There are numerous options under demographics, and you can select your own preferences if you choose to target your ads this way. Demographics relate to population traits, so you can set your ads to target people of a certain gender, race, nationality, age group, and so on.

- **Engagements:** If you choose to target ads based on engagement, it means that Facebook will show your ads to the people who like, comment, share, follow, tag, and react to your content. This method works well, but you will need the appropriate following to make the most of it.

- **Interests:** As implied, this method will find people on Facebook who have shown interest in similar brands, products, or niches to yours. For example, if you sell electric guitars Facebook will market your ads to people who have liked other guitar-related pages; from other music stores to rock music fan groups.

- **Location:** It's straightforward. You can aim your ads at people from or in a specific place. Facebook goes above and beyond though because you can narrow it down to your chosen zip code if you wanted to. You can also differentiate targeted ads by the locations people work, live in or check into.

- **Partner Connections:** Last, but not least, Facebook can target users based on how your business relates to them beyond their online personas. For example, if you sell car insurance Facebook may display your ad to new drivers, or people who recently took out a loan to buy a new car.

Doesn't that sound so much better than tagging your uncle in a business post, hoping he'll tell his friends about you? The coolest thing about this is that you don't have to pay for strategically placed billboards. Facebook delivers targeted ads straight to the user, with no extra intervention from you.

How to Set Up a Targeted Ad on Facebook

Once again, you'll have to optimize some settings in your Ads Manager to create a targeted ad. When you're logged in, select 'audiences' from the menu. The first thing you'll notice is that you can choose from three types: custom, lookalike, or saved.

Let's start with **custom audiences**. These are assumed to be the best for bringing in conversions as they're made up of your pre-existing clientele. In the event that you're not uploading a contact list, or handpicking the people you will advertise to, your pixel will scout those who have already shown interest in your business and target ads to them.

- **Step 1:** Select custom audience from the 'audiences' menu.

- **Step 2:** Choose how your audience will be defined. If you'd like to upload a contact or mailing list, choose "Customer File". Other options include "Web Traffic" if you'd like to use your pixel, "App Activity" if you want Facebook to target those who have already engaged your content (mostly apps and games that you've developed), and "Offline Activity" of you want to manually input the details of your customers. Select the most appropriate one for you.

- **Step 3:** If you've selected "Customer File", you'll have the option to import customer data from MailChimp, or to upload your own document. Pick the former and it's automatic, barring inputting your account details. Pick the latter, and you'll have to make sure that you upload a .TXT or .CSV file, otherwise Facebook won't be able to read it.

- **Step 4:** Upload your data, and then agree to Facebook's terms of use.

- **Step 5:** Facebook will generate a customer list. Take care with it, as some people report bugs in the system that confuse phone numbers for email addresses. If you need to edit any of the information, now's your chance, so take some time to go through it properly.

- **Step 6:** If everything is in order, select "Create Audience". It may take a while to update, but Facebook will notify you when it's ready to be used.

To create a **saved audience**, you'll need to know who you are targeting, because Facebook and its pixel won't be able to do the work for you. This can be done in a minute, maybe even less. All you have to do is:

- **Step 1:** Select "saved audience" from the 'audiences' menu.

- **Step 2:** Click on "Create A Saved Audience".

- **Step 3:** You'll see a form that you need to fill out to determine the demographics of your new audience. Input your preferred locations, genders, age-range, languages and other information. You can also name your audience at the top of the form.

- **Step 4:** Click "Create Audience". That's all you have to do. Your new target audience should appear in your list when you're finished setting it up. When next you produce an ad or promoted content, you'll be given the option to select or prioritize users that match your chosen demographics.

Next, we'll move on to **lookalike audiences**. Facebook describes a lookalike audience as a way to reach new people defined by their similarity to your existing audience ("Learn About Lookalike Audiences," 2019). The platform will pull common traits from your pixels, analytics and followers, find the common ground, and then target your content to others who have the same qualities. It's a powerful way to gain new customers, especially if you are a small business struggling for followers and engagement. To set one up for yourself, follow these steps:

- **Step 1:** Select "Lookalike Audience" from the Audiences menu.

- **Step 2:** You'll have to decide which audience your lookalike one will mimic. Choose from your custom or saved audiences.

- **Step 3:** Next, define the location and size of your lookalike audience by inputting your preferences. It will be a similar form to the one that pops up when creating a saved audience.

- **Step 4:** Click "Create Audience", and your lookalike customer base will be ready to go.

Tips and Tricks for Targeted Advertising on Facebook

Though it's ridiculously easy to set up targeted ads on Facebook, you shouldn't allow yourself to slack. Remember that doing the bare minimum is a rookie mistake for beginner marketers. If you want intermediate results, you're going to have to spend some more time on the administrative side of your marketing. There are a few good practices that you can implement to help you manage your ads, and perhaps even amplify their effects.

Experiment. Facebook is a large, brilliantly designed platform that has a lot of buttons you can press. If I tried to list every single option you have when it comes to optimization, this book would never end. Proceed with caution, of course, because you don't want to accidentally break Facebook or your ads, but nothing is stopping you from digging deeper and exploring the many levels of personalization Facebook has to offer.

Target by Life Event. This is one of the options you can use beyond setting your desired demographics or behaviors. Facebook will allow you to target customers based on what's happening in their lives, with emphasis on moving, new relationships, or developments like an engagement, anniversary, or family planning. This gives some businesses a gigantic advantage in targeted advertising. A good example would be a wedding venue targeting a newly engaged couple.

Maintain your leads and engagements. Loyalty and customer experience matter a lot more than growing empty likes. When people comment on your posts or ads, keep them interested by responding to them. Make an effort to answer their questions, or to direct them to the appropriate help pages. Just be careful not to feed the trolls. Report inappropriate comments on your posts, or if you have the power to, delete them yourself. Remember that your ads, posts and other content are an extension of your brand and you want to put your best foot forward in everything that you do.

Use complimentary apps. You don't have to rely solely on Facebook's analytics when it comes to advertising. There are a multitude of social media management apps, HootSuite being a popular all-in-one choice. You can find apps that will take care of your analytics, leads, schedule, notifications, SEO, and a lot more. Note that not all of the apps you find will be free, so you might have to make provision for them if you'd like to try them out or use them as part of your social media management.

Back to Basics

Even though you've now entered intermediate Facebook marketing, you might want to go back and rethink your initial strategy. You don't have to tear down and rebuild your marketing plan, but you should fill the gaps created when you designed your sales funnel without targeted ads, pixels, or the algorithm in mind.

When beginners start promoting their business on social media, they're bound to make mistakes and pour their energies into strategies that work on paper but not in practice. Usually it's the hustle technique, where the aim is to be seen by as many people as possible.

Raise your hand if any of your first few posts, be it on your business page or personal profile included unnecessary hashtags, links galore, or phrases like "Please share this. I'll be eternally grateful". Now raise your hand if you didn't go so overboard, but put in minimal effort, expecting the right people to find you without hashtagging everything or begging for support, but now you're struggling to be recognized by anyone at all.

I'm not criticizing you for either of those practices. They're easy traps to fall into, because rather than analyze what we're doing wrong and trying to figure out why these tips and tricks that are promoted don't work, we'll tell ourselves that it's a difficult market to break into, and we simply haven't struck lucky yet. That is nonsense. Unless you unintentionally went viral and now have millions of loyal followers, luck has nothing to do with it. Strategy is everything, and if yours is flimsy or flawed your business will suffer.

Advertising should be streamlined so that you don't look desperate and don't have to spend precious hours posting a million times a day for only four people, hoping they'll share it. Your ads should be appealing, but more importantly they should be placed and planned in such a way that those whom it appeals to will see it. The point of advertising is to get customers to come to you. There's no need to bombard your audience, and I suspect that you have some cleaning up to do.

So, if you really want to take your Facebook advertising to the next level there are a few things you'll have to do away with.

Stop adding links to your comment section

Some people believe that enticing viewers with links in the comments rather than the post itself will boost its visibility. There is little to no evidence that this works, and in fact, it could do more harm than good.

Firstly, as of 2020, there is no way to pin comments on Facebook. This means that you can't prioritize your own comments, so there's a risk that your link will be drowned out by other comments. It's so much safer to add links (if necessary) to the post itself.

Secondly, some people may interpret first comment links as scammy. There's something about it that seems a little bit unprofessional or suspect, and you could be scaring customers away. Link scams abound on Facebook, and I for one am not interested in clicking on strange, floating links in the comments just because a post told me to.

Don't believe that CTAs like this are effective. While there's nothing wrong with instructing people to check out your links to get more info or to be directed to a specific page, your execution of how you implement CTAs matters more than linking for the sake of it. Linking in your comments won't bypass the algorithm and it won't automatically boost your posts. I recommend that you refrain from doing so at all costs.

Stop Cross-Posting Between Facebook and Other Apps

It's wonderful that we can post something to one platform and share it directly to another. It's not so wonderful that doing so usually interferes with your post's display. Tweets look awesome on Twitter. Instagram photos stand out on Instagram. Youtube thumbnails look brilliant on Youtube. But when you cross-post, Facebook is guaranteed to throw off their formatting and make them look wonky.

It's not worth the three seconds you'll save in direct sharing between platforms. Instead, upload your content separately on each platform. Keep your hashtags and @'s on the platforms that are built for it, and focus on creating content that's appropriate and looks good on Facebook's engine. Your page will be so much neater and those who don't use other platforms won't be deterred by your post opening through a different app, website, or window.

Stop Tagging Irrelevant Accounts in Your Posts

This goes back to the idea of begging instead of advertising. Before you tag that person, page, or brand, stop and ask yourself why. Are they at all the subject of the post or promotion? Is the profile you're tagging relevant to your post or audience at all? If not, just don't do it.

For one, the person you're including may not want to be tagged in your ad, and if they request that you remove them from your post you are going to end up with egg on your face. For another, targeted advertising is meant to be subtle. You're not supposed to publicly target individual profiles directly. Instead, you should focus on demographics, otherwise your advertising will seem intrusive and unprofessional. You may also seem like you are trying to ride the coattails of others, or steal customers from them.

It's one thing to tag profiles of people who won a lucky draw you campaigned, or to thank someone for their efforts in a collaboration. It's a completely different thing to run an ad or promote a post, and then tag random people without their permission.

If you are convinced that the subject will appreciate your post, send them the link in a private message. Give them a choice to engage your post, otherwise you might annoy them and make yourself look bad.

Stop Engagement-Baiting People

Engagement-baiting is the practice of producing more-or-less empty content with the intention of goading people into reacting, or forcing reactions unnecessarily. Examples of this include those ever-annoying posts that demand you tag a friend so that they'll look at their phone for nothing, and marketing posts that present as surveys but in reality are just a cheap way to garner more likes, reactions, and shares than they deserve. I'm talking about posts that will say something like "Like for team Edward, share for team Jacob".

Sure, a lot of people will want to have their say and will take the bait, but as a marketer, what are you doing to grow your audience? A lot of people will see your post, but if it has nothing to do with your business, product, or service then what's the point? They're not going to pay attention to you or your brand, and at the end of the day you will have inaccurate impressions and false reach.

Not to mention that Facebook caught on and is now cracking down on engagement-bait (Morey, 2018). The algorithm is working to reduce the visibility of posts like this, as well as clickbait. You probably won't get into trouble for violating Facebook's terms of service if you choose to engage-bait, but it's a waste of time and an annoyance to a lot of people. It's not worth it.

Stop Using Personal Profiles for Business

We've all received friend requests from what's clearly a business profile. Maybe you've even set up a personal profile for your business. It's a genius idea, isn't it? You're guaranteed to interact with the people you befriend, your posts will have higher visibility, and it ups your branding game, right? Don't forget that it also cuts out the administration of operating a business page.

Maybe. But it's also illegal. To do so, you would have to set up your Facebook profile under a false name, and Facebook's community standards blatantly define doing so as misrepresentation ("Community Standards," n.d.).

Facebook hasn't really made an effort to remove such profiles, at least not any effort that I'm aware of, but the fact remains that doing business this way is a violation of Facebook's terms of service. If someone were to report you, or if Facebook otherwise caught on, your entire account (not just your profile, all attached pages, and admin) could be banned.

Furthermore, marketing yourself this way isn't as efficient as setting up a business page because of its drawbacks. If you have a profile you'll be limited to 5,000 friends, whereas on a page you can have infinite likes and followers. You also won't be able to gauge your support, because page likes count for something, while friend requests may not. A big problem is that you can't apply search engine optimisation to a profile, but you can to a page. If you set up a profile, you're limiting yourself to Facebook, and only one side of it at that.

Never, Ever, Buy Likes or Followers

Friendly reminder. Though it may be tempting to buy followers to boost your business page, this is one of the deadly sins of Facebook advertising (and indeed all social media marketing). If you have paid for a fanbase in the past, I'm sorry to say your best bet would be to cut your losses, delete your page, and start over again, for a number of reasons.

Once again, it violates Facebook's community standards as it falls under inauthentic content, spam, and misrepresentation (and I'm sure a dozen more violations). If you were to get caught, you'll likely face an immediate and permanent ban from the platform. Ethics come into play as well, and on a business note buying followers is the fastest way to shoot your business in its foot.

Even if it was an okay thing to do, buying likes won't boost your engagement. Facebook will feed your content to profiles that aren't real and can't engage you; or profiles that are real, but don't care. What's worse is that you won't be able to use targeted ads, because there won't be any basis for it (and again, even if there were, it would be ineffective).

Finally, it will make you look terrible. It's obvious when a page has purchased its following. If you have 20,000 likes or followers, but your shares, comments and other engagements average 50 at best, it's a dead giveaway that your following isn't real. People will know that you're dishonest, and you'll lose the faith of your audience.

Once you've righted all your wrongs, you'll have to do some upgrading as well. As mentioned, you'll have to rethink how you structure your Facebook business model. Before you start working on the actual ads you're going to put out there, make sure that you have covered all your bases for efficient and effective advertising on the platform.

The Takeaway

Optimization is everything, but you have to optimize your marketing according to the system that Facebook already has in place. Beginner marketers tend to advertise on Facebook without *using* Facebook as a tool. However, the platform is designed for socializing and its algorithm serves its users more than most realize. The objective is not to bypass the algorithm, but rather to use it to your advantage. On the flipside, if you don't understand the algorithm at all it could work against you and push your business into the void.

Pixels are another effective way to use Facebook's marketing power to its max. Though they are slightly controversial, as long as you have transparency and use the information they give your responsibly, you're in the clear.

Ultimately, whether you're using the algorithm, pixels, or simple content preferences to boost your business, they all tie into targeted advertising. Facebook is one of the best platforms to target audiences with, and doing so is streamlined for ease of use and efficiency.

Chapter 3: Modifying Your Medium

Don't worry, I promise my technical discussion of the Facebook machine is over... for now. In this chapter, we're going to have some fun with Facebook by moving on to what you're really here for: creating effective ads that make people engage. With the right approach, your ads will bring you new customers and allow your business to grow and expand through Facebook.

Now, you don't have to go and get a Ph.D. in advertising or design to create stunning ads that will drive sales. A little creativity will go a long way and work wonders for your brand. However, you can't go into this with half a mind or heart. So before you jump straight into creating your next campaign, let's take a look at some of the avenues that you can explore to do so.

Facebook is a flexible platform that offers various means of advertising. It would be a shame to lose out on advertising opportunities by not wielding each of them to their full capacity. You don't have to use every trick listed in this chapter, but remember that you have room to experiment, and there's no harm in testing the waters before you learn how to swim.

Beginner marketers often place more emphasis on having an abundance of ads rather than focusing on creating quality promotional content. Even if you only have one single campaign running, if you do it well it might just be enough to boost your business. There are certain things you'll have to keep in mind when you design (or redesign) your ads. So what makes a good ad, and more importantly, what qualifies as an effective ad on Facebook?

Advertising has been around for a long, long time—much longer than you'd think. The first print ad appeared during the 15th century in a book (Siddigui Jr, 2010). It's no surprise that once printed media became popular it changed into a marketing tool and newspapers, magazines, and all that came after followed suit. Back then, ads simply detailed why buyers should choose one brand over another, or explained why you were a fool for not buying this necessary product that would keep you safe instead of sorry. Ads tried to be entertaining so as to stand out, captivate, and be memorable, but facts were front and center. Ads were somewhat low effort and got to the point immediately.

No one can really say when the advent of modern advertising truly began because the concept of it was a long time coming. Regardless, by almost all accounts, advertising as we know it began in the 1920s. That is when ads changed to be more than just an exchange of information. With society focused on glitz and glamour, and every person chasing the American Dream and idolizing the faces of commercialism, ads became campaigns. Led by high society models, celebrity personalities, and icons of the decade, the message of advertising was no longer "You need this, buy it". It was now "You *want* to buy this, and if you don't, maybe you suck".

The 1920s was the point in history when advertising became competitive because brand power meant everything. The ads you see today—of high rollers enjoying an ice cold beer, or supermodels gathering around a pleasant smelling man—work off of that same blueprint. People are more inclined to spend money on what they want than what they need. You've experienced this. Surely you've complained that you have to pay for textbooks or a doctor's appointment, but have had no trouble splurging on a new game console, nice clothes, or a trip abroad. As an advertiser, your job is to make people *want* to throw money at you.

Let's use health as a silly example. Say there are two competing brands of slimming supplements. Brand

A advertises their product by listing all the benefits of losing weight, down to the scientific proof. Brand B advertises their product using a slim, beautiful person easily slipping into a tight outfit. Their hook is something along the lines of "this could be you". Which brand do you think will make more money in the end? The answer is Brand B, because they're showing you what you want and then telling you that they can give it to you.

There's a brilliant line from the *Mad Men* pilot that comes to mind (Taylor, 2007). In the midst of a declining customer base for cigarettes thanks to new evidence that smoking kills, Don Draper and his team of advertisers have to come up with a way to market the very thing that no one wants to buy anymore. In an effort to prevent Lucky Strike from pulling away from the company, Draper—in a moment of utter desperation—thinks of the (real-life) slogan "It's toasted". When Lucky Strike's representatives argue that all cigarettes are toasted, Draper says, *"No. Everybody else's tobacco is poisonous. Lucky Strike is toasted."*

It's a powerful scene that rings true in the real world. In the 100 or so years since modern advertising took the reins, nothing has changed. If you want to be effective in your advertising, you're going to have to be competitive. You could spend all your money and time on a professional ad that spreads to all 2.5 billion people on Facebook. If your ad doesn't make people care, it will be worthless.

Though you don't need to study advertising to be an advertiser, you need to respect the fact that effective advertising is both a talent and a skill. You can't place any old nonsense ad on Facebook and expect to make money from it. You'll have to start by understanding how ads work on Facebook, and learning the tricks of the trade.

The Versatility of Facebook

If you remember only one thing from this chapter, let it be this: Facebook is a multimedia platform, and so your advertising has to match that. It's one of the best things about promoting yourself on the platform. Your options aren't as limited as they would be on other networks where one medium dominates over others. Look at Instagram and images, Youtube and videos, and Twitter and text. If you were to see a text ad on Youtube it would be out of place. Most people don't go to Youtube to read. If your ad has no sound or movement, it won't do very well on the platform.

On Facebook, however, you can do whatever you like. If you prefer a photographic ad to get started, it will fit right in. If you'd rather have a flyer, it will blend well into people's timelines. So will videos, and so will text promos. Each has its place on the platform, all you have to do is learn how to work with them.

The problem comes in when you consider that different people will pay attention to different things. Maybe the millenials on Facebook enjoy ads in videos more than flyers featured in their feeds. Older generations might enjoy reading. If you're advertising muscle cars to traditional men, you won't want to have an overtly cute, bright, and "girly" poster, because it likely won't appeal to your target audience. Likewise, if you're advertising a video game to Gen Z, why on earth wouldn't you include a high-energy video demonstration of its gameplay?

Before you even start designing your ad, you're going to have to put a fair amount of thought into who the ad is intended for. Of course, taking the steps in the previous chapter will help you immensely with this.

When your target audience is defined and you have an idea of what sort of content they'll find appealing, you must also consider how they're experiencing the bulk of what they see online. If your pixels show that your clientele are more likely to click on video ads than they are any other format, you'll have to keep up with them on that.

But then you'll also have to think about which devices your target market uses as different screens require different ad specs. If you've created a poster that doesn't fit on a mobile screen, your audience will probably scroll right past it. It won't matter to them at all that your ad looks perfect on a laptop or tablet. Think about it, Gen Z probably aren't using laptops to engage you, so if you were to promote a video game to them as your target demographic, you'd have to make sure that your ad looks good on mobile screens, because that's where they're most likely to stumble upon it.

One last consideration is that ads can be multimedia too. Shake things up, it won't hurt you at all. A photo or poster with a cool SEO friendly caption will look good and appeal to those who like pictures and words. A gallery containing a flyer and a video is bound captivate and entertain if the content is good. Uniformity has its place, but if all of your ads are the same format, advertising the same business or product with the same slogan, theme, and point then they're going to stagnate. Be careful that your customers don't take on a "seen one, seen them all" attitude towards your promotions.

You don't have to try them all at once, but I encourage you to give each medium a go if you can. Here's a brief look at each advertising option available to you before we dive into their depths:

- **Boosted posts:** These are by far the simplest way to promote your business. Technically, they're not really ads. A Boosted post is a regular post of any format that you've paid to promote to a wider audience. These work well for plain text.

- **Images:** The easiest way to get your image ads out there is to add pictures to your posts before you boost them as described above. You don't have to add a text caption if you don't want to.

- **Videos:** Slightly more time consuming to produce well, video ads are powerful because of their near limitless possibilities. From scripted footage, to animation, to infomercial style demos or trailer-like snippets, there is a lot of room to play with these.

- **Carousel ads:** The objective of a carousel is to showcase a gallery of images or videos that users can slide through. They're more dynamic than single object ads, and can be set up to create a panorama effect. They're excellent for advertising ranges and services.

- **Slideshows:** Easy to compile in your Ads Manager, these are exactly what they sound like. They're short videos containing a series of still images, videos, and/or text. The biggest pro is that they're not production heavy and use less bandwidth. This means that they load faster and conserve data.

- **Collections:** These work best for suppliers and manufacturers of physical goods. Using a collection ad, you can showcase up to five products that viewers can scroll through and purchase instantly through the ad.

There are other types of ads that you can choose from. In some cases they're too specific and complicated to cover in detail in this chapter, while in others, they're simple enough to understand without further details or emphasis. This includes experience ads, playable ads, and lead ads.

Beyond the different mediums that you can explore you also have to think about ad placement. On Facebook's primary platform your ads can feature in user feeds, be placed before videos, or be part of Stories. Ads can also be placed in Messenger.

Dynamic ads are optimized to target chosen audiences and will be boosted to the people most likely to engage them. They can be any format or type, and are a fantastic way to retarget existing customers.

As you can see, you have a lot of choices when it comes to marketing on Facebook. How do you make the most of each one, and which is best for your business needs? The only way to determine that is to read on and learn more about each type of ad.

Boost Your Posts

Sometimes you just won't feel like jumping through hoops to create a brilliant ad. Maybe you'd rather post something simple that your audience can engage—a press release, announcement, event or poll for example. They're a great way to market job opportunities, launch parties, surveys, promotions and pretty much everything else.

Boosting your posts is by far the easiest way to reach more people on Facebook. There aren't any specs you'd have to meet (unless you're boosting an image or video attachment), posts can be created in seconds, and you can choose the audience you'd like to boost your post to.

Keep in mind that although you can set your boosted post to appear for interested new customers, they're far more efficient at catering to the audience that you already have. A boosted post will take priority in your followers' feeds, so they're best used for retargeting or for marketing news, events, giveaways, and promos that your clientele are likely to engage.

Don't underestimate the power of a boosted post. Since your post will spread faster and further but remain in Facebook's feed as it would under ordinary circumstances, you should put effort into creating a post that's shareable. Your audience will boost it even more if they choose to hit the share button and if they do, your post will get even more reach than you originally bargained for. For this reason, boosted posts are perfect for raising brand awareness.

If you're pressed for time but need to get some marketing in, boosting a post is the best option. Look at how easy it is.

How to Boost a Post

Naturally, you will have to be logged in to the account you want to boost a post from. The cool thing is that you don't have to navigate through your Ads Manager because boosted posts aren't considered advertisements. Once you're in, follow these steps.

- **Step 1:** Create a new post or find an old that you want to promote. Don't forget to spellcheck if you're boosting a text post.

- **Step 2:** Add your desired images, videos or other media (if you want to).

- **Step 3:** Click the "Boost Post" button at the bottom right corner of your post. If you don't see it, you may have to share your post first and return to it later to continue.

- **Step 4:** Fill in the important information regarding your boosted post. You can select the audience you want to boost it to, how long you want to boost it for, your budget for your boost campaign and your payment method.

- **Step 5:** When you're all done and ready to go, hit the "Boost Post" button on screen.

Tips for Boosting Posts

You may be tempted to boost any and all posts that you can, but you must resist the urge to. Even though boosted posts aren't ads by definition, you should still treat them as though they were. Remember that your posts will appear to more people, so if you do half a job or create posts that don't serve your business, it could damage your brand.

It goes without saying then that your post should be appealing and audience-friendly. If it's only text, stick to important updates or promos. Don't boost every thought that comes into your head. If you do, your followers might not engage your post at all, and even if they do, you won't be building your business if you're promoting nonsense instead of driving sales or creating leads.

Use boosted posts wisely. If you boost too many, you risk flooding your audience's feed, and they may become irritated and unfollow or hide your posts and page.

Think about when you're going to boost your post too. You'll want your post to spread when there is the highest chance of people seeing it. This is especially important if you're attempting to pull in more customers. You'll have to do some research, but it will be well worth it.

As for creating an engaging post, one trick is to have a look at your insights on your Facebook Business page. There, you'll find the stats of all your posts and it will give you a good idea of which posts were well received and worth mimicking (or boosting if it's appropriate). For example, if you can see that posts with GIF images have the most engagement, add a GIF to the post you'd like to boost.

Beyond this, make sure that your post demands interaction from those who see it. Don't just boost a picture of a heart with the caption "Happy Valentine's Day". Include a CTA, a link that leads to your website, or more information about a special Valentine's Day deal. Don't force empty likes either (refer back to my warning about engagement-baiting). Remember that the purpose of boosting a post is to broaden your clientele. You'll waste money if your post serves no purpose.

Make your post entertaining, eye-catching, captivating or even just noticeable. How you do this is up to you. It could be a funny post that leads to a discount link. The picture you add could be bright and popping. Perhaps it's a campaign for a cause you care about and you'll add a dramatic video explaining why people should join you on your mission.

Be creative. At the end of the day a boosted post is still just a post. If it doesn't stand out, it won't be effective. The rest—like whether to boost an event, giveaway, job listing, or promo—is up to you.

Image Ads

Pictures are a dominant force on Facebook, and learning how to work with them is a prerequisite for effective advertising. According to Hubspot, posts containing visuals are 40 times more likely to be shared by Facebook users (Andrews, 2017). Posts with relevant images are also 94% more effective and viewed than posts with random images that don't tie in so well.

Adding visuals to your posts is also a trend in marketing, so if you want to compete or keep up, you're going to have to up your visual game. One survey showed that marketers use visuals in almost 100% of their posts. The survey also noted that 35% of marketers prefer images—stock photos in particular—over all other types of visuals (Ekine, 2017).

Adding photos to your posts—boosted, ads, or otherwise—is one of the best ways to capture the attention of people scrolling by. If your picture is loud, viewers are more likely to take notice of it. Images and advertising have gone hand in hand since humans figured out that illustrations added that extra bit of *pizazz* to their printed words. Photos have featured in ads since the 1800s, when the first cameras came to be (Rothkopf, 2014). Only behind text, pictures have dominated advertising the longest out of all the mediums. Think about it. Images are used for marketing in magazines and other printed media (books, flyers, posters, pamphlets, brochures, etc.), on billboards, banners, book covers, and packaging, and even on TV when combining video and stills. Facebook isn't exempt from the power of visual marketing, and pictures are the best place to start.

There are two ways that you can create and share image-based ads on Facebook. The first would be to add a picture, photo, infographic, or other still visual to a regular post and then boost it as described in the previous section. The second is to create an official ad from scratch to release it through your Ads Manager.

Setting Up Your Image

The most important factor here is the dimensions of your image. If you mess this up, your ad won't display properly and won't be effective. This is what

Facebook itself recommends ("Facebook Image Ad Specs," 2019):

Format: jpg or png.

Dimensions for desktop: Minimum 476 (w) x 249 (h) pixels.

Dimensions for mobile: Minimum 320 (w) pixels.

Resolution: Highest possible resolution is recommended, minimum 1080 x 1080 pixels if ad is linked.

Image Ratio: 1.91:1 to 4:5 (recommended), 1.91:1 to 1:1 (with link).

Panorama ads and 360 images are automatically optimized by Facebook's machines so you don't have to worry about their dimensions if you use them. Facebook will also allow you to use the same single image across desktop and mobile, but you'll have to make sure that its dimensions will look good on both.

Designing Your Ad

Start by figuring out which picture you will use. So long as your image is of high enough quality, nothing is stopping you from using your own photos or designs. If, however, you don't have pictures of your own that are worthy, try scouting royalty free (for commercial use) stock photos. If you're willing to pay, Shutterstock is a leader, but there are free options too, like Pixabay and Unsplash. When choosing a photo, keep the following in mind:

- Facebook has a 20% text rule for images, meaning that the algorithm will reject ads containing more words than this allocation (Vrountas, 2016). If you're creating your ad on Facebook, its tools will make it easier for you to gauge if your ad is acceptable or not. Regardless, you will have to plan your ad so that it's optimized for minimal reading. Remember that your ad is meant to be eye-catching, so you wouldn't want a wall of text in it anyway.

- It's a myth that successful ads require certain elements like babies, animals or smiling people. This is only logical, as relevancy matters. Why would you want to use a picture of a smiling family on vacation if you're a funeral home? A picture of a cute dog doesn't add any value if you're marketing handmade jewelry. Keep your images in line with what you're promoting. Your audience will notice it first, so it really should say a thousand words.

- Make your image ad informative. If you're promoting a limited time offer, make sure that the numbers are in the ad and easy to spot. Add your logo, so people can identify your brand even if they're not paying attention to your account or caption. If a CTA is included, make it obvious. Your ad should be easily absorbed in little time. This works well with the 20% rule too. If customers have to read paragraphs to figure out what you're promoting, your ad will probably be a dud.

- Don't forget to make your ad appealing to your target audience. If you try to stand out too much, your ad may be obscure and fly over people's heads.

- If you don't want any text in your ad, add a caption to your post. Your audience won't be able to smell what you're advertising. Make it as obvious as possible, even if it's not featured in the image itself.

- If you're no good at design, there are tools that can help you. Canva is the most popular one today, and has preset dimensions for your Facebook needs. You can find free images that you can combine, alter, or adjust. Its drag and drop interface means there's little to learn before you get it right, and each of its fonts are designed to be aesthetically pleasing. You can pay for premium content if you like. Otherwise, you always have the option to hire a graphic designer. More on that later, though.

Creating an Image Ad

You can choose if you'd like to set up a quick ad or a guided ad. If you choose the latter, Facebook will show you exactly what to do and how to do it, so it's recommended if you haven't quite found your feet in your Ads Manager. The steps you take will look like this:

- **Step 1:** From your Ads Manager, select "Create Campaign"

- **Step 2:** Fill in the necessary information. Name your campaign, define your budget strategy, and select your ad's objective from Facebook's list. Note that there are advanced options in this section of set up. You can play around with delivery, scheduling and optimisation if you so desire.

- **Step 3:** Now to define your ad set. Here, you'll set your budget, target audience, ad placement, duration and delivery preferences.

- **Step 4:** Create your ad. You will have to input the associated Page that it will run from, the format (choose single image from the list), the media you're using, and the text you'd like to add if necessary. Facebook will bring up a design window that you can experiment in. When you're done, hit "Preview" to double check that your ad looks good.

- **Step 5:** If you confirm your ad, payment for it will be deducted from your account. If it's the first time you have placed an ad on Facebook, you will have to input your billing information.

- **Step 6:** Once your ad is ready and your payment checks out, your ad will be live on Facebook and other platforms you selected when you defined your placement specifications.

If you choose to create a quick ad, most of these steps remain the same. However, you will have the option to create a new ad for a pre-existing campaign. It takes less time, but you won't get the walkthrough of what to do. You can switch between the two modes, or save your work as a draft for later.

Video Ads

Though still images have dominated marketing since the dawn of advertising, videos have caught up. One survey reported that 52% of participating marketers prefer video to stills when using visual media in advertising (Dopson, 2019). The survey also showed that an overwhelming 59.3% of marketers experienced more engagement and clicks with video ads than they did when using pictures. The theory is that videos are set up to push engagement because a viewer can't get the necessary information with a quick glance. This entices viewers to stay and watch instead of scrolling past. There isn't solid proof in favor of this, but it is a logical assumption.

Like images, video ads have been around for a while. The first of its kind—a campaign for Bulova watches—aired in 1941 during a baseball game. It lasted for 10 seconds. This practice, of putting video ads in between other content (and so keeping it short and sweet) continues to this day. In fact, the standard for placed ads on Facebook is 10 seconds.

Let's not sugarcoat video ads, though. They may be effective, and thanks to television and platforms like YouTube, they're considered a staple. But if you don't have the means to create a good video ad they're best left alone.

Creating a video ad isn't as simple as downloading a royalty free picture from the internet, smacking your logo onto it and paying Facebook to spread it for you. Video ads will demand time to create, and you might have to spend money on hiring a professional if you don't know what you're doing.

On the bright side, video ads are extremely versatile, so you're bound to find a style or method that works for you. Like images, you can use stock footage (either free or paid), and soundtracks or voiceovers. If you're not interested in the latter, you can overlay text to get your point across instead. You can film a professional video, put together an animation, or combine footage and stills for dramatic effect. There's no need to purchase professional software either. Videos can be produced online, or even on your phone with the right app. Regardless of how you put your ad together, execution is everything. Here's what you should know:

How to Make a Good Video Ad

Think about the ads you've seen on video platforms, and which ones you enjoyed, which ones worked and which ones you wish you could unsee. Video ads can be extremely irritating if you don't do them properly. Unlike an image you can scroll past, sometimes there is no escape from placed ads.

Often, they disrupt content, so if your ad isn't good, or is even remotely annoying, your audience will hate it.

To prevent this, implement the following strategies and elements that will make your video ad as bearable, entertaining and enjoyable as possible.

- Consider silence. If you're placing your video ad in people's feeds, they might autoplay. If they're obnoxiously loud, contain irritating jingles, or use repetitive phrases that will stagnate after the first time a viewer hears it, the audio in your video might deter people from it. There's also a chance that users have their autoplay set to mute, and will miss your audio if their sounds are off. Keep in mind that a lot of people browse Facebook at work, on public transport, in waiting rooms, and other places where noise may be inappropriate. Some users might also have earphones in and you don't want your ad to deafen them. Audio isn't terrible, and you are welcome to use it if that's what you want. Just don't do so thoughtlessly. Consider the implications if you do.

- Remember it's an online ad, not a feature film. No one, and I mean no one, wants to watch an ad that goes on for ten years. This is especially important if you are placing your ads before or during other videos on the platform. Keep your video ads short and get to the point. Facebook ads are often unskippable. If your ads are boring, and don't wrap up quickly, you may have to face viewers blocking all ads from you just to avoid them.

- Put effort into it. Don't even think about producing video ads that have shoddy audio or low quality footage. This is one area that you really cannot afford to skimp on. Imagine if TV ads were low, 3GP quality with distorted voice overs. Video ads work when they're sophisticated. Quality is everything. Go for the highest resolution that you possibly can, and if you are using a voice over, have it professionally recorded.

- Even if you are not filming anything, create a script (or storyboard) for your ad. Don't wing it. If you are creating the ad yourself, having a reference or blueprint will make its production so much easier. If you're using captions, or overlaying text in any way, plan out what your video will say. You don't want your ad to look unprofessional, and good ads have good planning behind them.

- There are many services you can use to create videos from scratch. If you'd like to go the DIY route but with professional software, consider using Adobe Premiere Pro and After Effects. There will be a learning curve, but you can create high quality productions with them. A free alternative is DaVinci Resolve. There are countless websites that allow you to drag and drop video elements for animations, or even to produce your own videos from photos and footage without downloading software to your computer. Remember you can use mobile apps too, though they may not be as easy to work with. Shy away from platforms that will watermark your work. It's better to pay to remove them, or to find alternative software. Remember that this is your ad. Don't promote other businesses in them (unless that's the point).

- Facebook recommends videos that are either .mov or MP4 formats. They should have a resolution of at least 720p and can't be bigger than 2.3 gigabytes. The recommended aspect ratio is 16:9 for widescreens.

- If all else fails, hire someone to do it for you. You can find affordable creators online, or even hire freelancers if it's easier for you. It will make a difference in both the quality and effect of your ad.

Video Ad Placement

You also need to think about where your video ad is going to go. Choose wisely, as ad placement could affect engagement, depending on your audience. The type of ad you use also factors into this. For example, a loud, repetitive ad that disrupts content won't be well received. A slideshow on the sidebar but be easily overlooked. It's up to you, but it's recommended that you choose from one of two placements.

News Feed ads stand the highest chance of pulling conversions because your audience is more likely to see and engage it. They're not as invasive as other video ads and won't be out of sight and overshadowed by sitting on the side. One drawback is that if you use sound, as mentioned above, your audience might not be fully impacted by it if their autoplay is set to mute. Another is that viewers can easily scroll past it if they're not interested.

In Stream ads are the ones that feature alongside other content. You can set your ad to pre-roll, mid-roll, or post-roll, meaning that it will play before, during, or after someone else's video. They're excellent for brand awareness, but generally speaking aren't as effective at conversions as News Feed ads are. There's also a risk of annoying viewers with disruptive ads that are unskippable or unappealing to them.

There are more placement options available, like the right column, but these work better for images or banner ads. Another thing you could try is to promote your ad as a suggested video, though it's better to save this option for organic video content rather than advertising purposes.

How to Set Up a Video Ad

By now, you should know how to set up and optimize an ad. Creating a video ad follows similar steps to image ads, with the exception that you'll be able to create one from scratch using Facebook's interface.

- **Step 1:** When creating a new ad, select "Get video views" as your objective.

- **Step 2:** As with your other ads, define your budget, audience, schedule, and other metadata.

- **Step 3:** Create your ad. You can build one from nothing or upload a video to the platform here. If you choose the latter, make sure that it matches Facebook's specs. If you're creating a video, select the footage you'd like to use from the library. If you like you can create a slideshow using still images as well.

- **Step 4:** Add a caption to your video ad if you want to. This will be the copy that features above your video in people's timelines, so take care with it.

- **Step 5:** Preview your video before you post it. As with other ads, if it's all ready to go and you're happy with the final product, confirm publishing it and Facebook will take care of the rest.

Mixed Media Ads

There's no need to give you the step-by-step instructions for setting up multimedia ads. In the case of videos, your text, images and audio make up the film, so setting it up follows the instructions in the previous section. Slideshow ads become videos, so again, the steps are the same. As for carousel and collection ads, all you have to do is follow the same steps for setting up an image ad campaign, but instead of choosing "single image", you'll select either of the two from the list. You will be able to arrange the media in the order you'd like it to appear in, and you'll be able to add or edit the captions that will appear below them.

The premise of each one is the same: instead of using one single piece of media (or a single medium), you can use multiple and separate images, videos, or both in one single ad. Your audience will be able to scroll (flip) through each one, and so you can showcase more than one product, page or service without running more than one ad.

There are a few considerations for each one that sets it apart from the rest. Let's start with the carousel.

How to Create a Cool Carousel

Carousel ads are best for showcasing what you have to offer. They're highly effective at driving engagement and sales, with some reports claiming that they're 10 times more successful than static ads on Facebook (Enrico, n.d.). Carousels are handy if you sell or provide miscellaneous products and services, and would like to show people your business' many facets. Even if you only sell a single product, carousel ads can help you promote it. Each panel can be used to describe, explain, or promote a different aspect of your product, or you can use the extra panels to drive leads to your website or mailing list. When creating a carousel ad, keep the following good practices in mind:

Quality over quantity is important. There is no point in having a thousand panels if they're all bad, uninformative, irrelevant, repetitive, or dull. Stick to what you need the carousel for. Don't try to force extra panels in there to make it look cooler. If you don't have enough content to fill an entire carousel, perhaps you should consider a single image ad or a slideshow instead.

Your carousel should tell a story. Each panel should connect to each other and be seamless when people slide through them. The best carousels represent a single idea, like what your business does, the products you produce, services you can offer, where to find you, how your service works, and so on. You could add one of each idea, but you must make sure that the panels will gel together just as well as they stand alone. Don't neglect your captions or headlines either.

Experiment. Try combining images and videos in the carousel. It will make your ad more dynamic and it's an opportunity to fit more information in one single ad. You can also play around with the order of the panels, and even optimize it using the creation tool. If you want to get really creative, you could create panorama carousels in which each panel shows a segment of the same picture, to create a continuous image throughout the ad. Or, you could try to split your text over each panel, so that they create one sentence or question that ends with the carousel. Remember that although carousels are eye-catching, your audience must still be motivated to browse them. Carousels are no exception to working at garnering and retaining viewer attention.

Add your info. Carousels work best when you're showcasing what you've got, but they can still generate leads and conversions. Add your contact info, mailing list sign up, website, landing page, or links to your store to your panels too. Some people add their info at the end of the carousel; others link contact information to each one. It's up to you.

Creating Conversions Through Collections

Collection ads are best if you're trying to drive sales. The objective is that your products or services (to a lesser degree) will be displayed and available for purchase or browsing directly from the ad. If you are not necessarily selling something and would rather promote yourself and what you do, a carousel ad is a better option. If you have a range of products with set prices and you can't fit them into a single image or cover them all in a video or boosted post, collection ads are the best solution for you. You still need to put some thought or preparation into your collection ads as the display and discovery of them could affect engagement and potential sales.

It's a good idea to **showcase your most popular items first**. Facebook's algorithm sets and customizes this for you, so it's made easy. If you'd rather handpick your featured items you're welcome to, but Facebook will prioritize your items based on their appeal and which items are likely to see the most sales.

You should have a catalogue too. This way, if customers are interested in other items of yours you can refer them to it by linking to your inventory or store. Facebook will also automatically fill your collection with the next best items if your featured products sell out, or don't suit the algorithm.

Don't display repetitive products. Your collection should be a taste of your business. You want people to purchase what they see, but you also want them to explore further and potentially spend more money in buying more from you. If you showcase the same product five times over, your business will seem limited and customers might not be motivated to dig deeper. Add some variety, and don't forget to link your viewers to your main store, website or page.

If you have models or scenes in your photos, **identify your products in the image**. Facebook recommends this, and it could generate more engagement and leads. If you are using models or other lifestyle images, throw in some of your items that aren't displayed in the collection ad. This will nurture further discovery and will generate leads and traffic to your catalogue.

Facebook Ad FAQ

When dealing with any type of ad, remember that you don't have to stick with methods that don't work. If you find that video ads aren't nearly as effective as image ads are, you are not bound to continue using them. Everyone's audience is different and it will take a lot of trial and error before you hit your advertising sweet spot. Don't be afraid to experiment, and don't shy away from cutting your losses and moving on when your ads don't work as well as you hoped they would. Creating effective ad campaigns is a skill. The more you practice, the better at it you will become.

Still, it's not unusual for many entrepreneurs to have some concerns when it comes to running ads. The following are the most popular questions about

Facebook advertising and how much you should invest in it.

How Much Money Should You Spend on Facebook Ads?

You may not like it, but there is no formula to how much you should budget for. The cool thing about Facebook is that you can control how much you spend on ads by limiting how far they spread. This way, you aren't paying for space and time that you don't occupy, and won't be swindled into spending extra money on ineffective advertising.

Your need for advertising is something only you can determine. You will have to create your own budget, based on your own business needs. Facebook ads shouldn't be your only means of marketing, so remember to budget for other campaigns as well. You can also test the waters before you commit more money to your Facebook marketing. Start small and pay attention to your analytics to see if it makes a difference. If it does, you'll know that it was money well spent and can plan to invest more into Facebook ads later.

Should You Hire Professionals?

Look, there is really no need to pay someone to manage your ads for you unless you are swamped and have no time to handle your own social media, or you are so technologically disadvantaged that Facebook feels like rocket science to you. There are perks to hiring content managers, and they'll likely do a stellar job of your self-promotion, but if you are a small business you can save money by doing all of this yourself. Facebook's Ads Manager is simple and easy to navigate and to reiterate, the more you use it, the better at using it you will become.

But then there's the issue of whether you should hire a professional to create the ads themselves. This also depends entirely on you. Do you trust yourself to create excellent ads? Go ahead and take care of it yourself if you do. But if you are a total amateur in design, aren't very good at writing catchy headlines, and don't know the first thing about video production, trust me, the money you spend on pros will save you a world of pain and embarrassment.

It's not to say that either is better. My point is that quality is everything in advertising, especially online. If you are unable to produce quality marketing material, you could shoot your own business in the foot.

Are There Free Ways to Advertise on Facebook?

Yes… and no. If you want to get technical, then it's the latter. Facebook does not have free options for official ads. If you want boosted content, whether it's a post or a full-scale ad, you're going to have to pay up. That said, there are ways that you can market for free on Facebook.

Most of the elementary tricks you learned will still apply. So long as you don't resort to engagement-baiting, breaking Facebook's rules, or trying to game the algorithm there are many free, quick, and efficient ways that you can promote yourself without paying.

There are too many tips to cover, but I'm talking about things like:

- Posting regularly to stay relevant and seen.
- Inviting people to like and support your page the good old-fashioned way.
- Word of mouth (through chats and comments, or recommendations to your products and services when it's appropriate).
- Scheduling your posts for optimal visibility.
- Creating shareable content that your customers will enjoy and engage.

- Linking to your Facebook page, website or store on other social media platforms (like Twitter or Instagram).
- Creating free content on other platforms (for example, a YouTube channel or a blog).

These strategies work if you implement them properly. You can't expect to make money or gain followers from your videos if they're low quality and infrequent. If you don't want to spend money on advertising, you're going to have to put time and effort into it instead.

The Takeaway

Facebook advertising is one of the most efficient ways that you can put your business out there, but only if you understand that it's not "one size fits all". There are so many options available to you, from boosting simple posts you wish more people would see, to producing scripted promo videos in a studio. You have to figure out which ones work best for your business on your own because no two audiences are the same and what works for me, might be a complete dud for you. Furthermore, using only type of advertising on a platform as wide as Facebook is a bit silly, don't you think?

Ultimately, Facebook ads are easy to set up and run no matter the medium, but they are serious business. It may be necessary to hire professional designers and producers, as they'll have a better understanding of what works and what doesn't. You can take the DIY route, but be aware that if you don't understand advertising, you might just set yourself up for failure. If that's the case, boosting your content is a great alternative to full-scale ads.

Chapter 4: Facebook Mobile

I solemnly swear that the difficult part is behind us. From here on out, there'll be less instruction and more discussion. We've covered how Facebook delivers ads and how you can go about creating ads that suit its engine, but what about how your ads are received? If you don't think about how users will experience your final product, you might allow mistakes to slip through the cracks.

The reality is that Facebook is used on many different devices in many, many different ways. The most popular means are with a computer or laptop (the desktop version), or through the mobile app (Facebook mobile). That's not where it ends. Some users visit Facebook through browsers on their phone. Generally, it will mimic the app, but it's not so streamlined and there is always the option to switch to desktop through a mobile browser which isn't easy on the eyes or optimized for ease of use. Then you have users logged on through tablets, and some who will experience Facebook's joys through other smart devices like TVs or game consoles.

This raises one problem. Just because you have

created a dashing ad on your end, it doesn't mean that it looks good on the user's end. Your input isn't always your output and in marketing this matters more than you know.

Facebook's Demographics

So, what are we dealing with? Yes, you should keep mobile app users in mind, but how important is it to cater to them when you're marketing and promoting your business? To answer this, let's look at the stats.

According to one report from February 2020, there are 1.47 billion active desktop users. By comparison, there are 2.26 billion active mobile users. Allow me to drive this home. That's 96% of Facebook's entire population (Salman Aslam, 2019). If you aren't optimizing your ads for Facebook mobile, I'm sorry, but you might as well not advertise at all.

This opens up an entire world of consideration, and you may have to rethink your marketing strategy to make room for the majority. In a perfect world, you should create ads that work perfectly on all screens. Unfortunately, this is the real world, and here, it's too unpredictable. Your ad could look absolutely stunning on one phone, and utterly wonky on another. Different screens have different settings, and if you try to design your ads for all of them, it's guaranteed you will lose your mind in the process.

So, my first recommendation is to focus on three things: Facebook Mobile (the app specifically), the desktop version, and tablet screens, in that order. Don't worry about what your ad looks like through an Xbox or a smart microwave because although users can access Facebook through such ridiculous devices, they're not going to. No one thinks, "Gotta update my status, let me just pop over to my TV". Even if there are such people in existence, they are the minority—one so insignificant it doesn't count.

Next, you'll have to think about which types of ads, and which placements work best on which screens.

Honestly, figuring this out is mostly a matter of logic. If you place an ad in the right column or side bar, mobile users won't see it because the app doesn't have a sidebar. Likewise, although carousel ads work well on all screens, sliding through them is so much easier on a touchscreen than would be with a mouse or a keyboard. Your design matters too. For example, small words won't be as easy to read on a mobile screen, but sharing posts across apps works best on mobiles, because Facebook, Messenger, WhatsApp, Instagram, and other apps are all interconnected and often use the same account or email address. Also, flyers, posters or still images look amazing on desktop because they'll fit nicely on the screen and won't get cut off if they're too big.

One more thing that you must keep in mind is that it's far easier to block ads on computers than it is to block them on phones. It would be a shame if you put hours of effort into producing an ad that people won't even see.

Ultimately, you can use whichever mediums you like, regardless of the screens you're designing them for. So long as you understand how the user will view and experience your ad, and stick to the recommended dimensions, everything will be just fine.

Optimizing Ads for All Screens

Speaking of dimensions, I've covered the most important ones in the previous section, but I will say that when you're designing your ads in Facebook or on platforms like Canva your workspace will be preset, or you'll have a guideline or reminder of the dimensions you should be working with. In most cases, when you preview your ad you'll get a glimpse of how it will display on various screens.

I just wanted to note that the only way to optimize your ads for different screens is to design them for different screens. Unfortunately, there isn't any way around this, and the best way to avoid shoddy ads across all platforms is to host different campaigns for different devices.

Yes, it will cost you a little bit more to maintain, but it's better than risking damage to your brand because your ad looks stupid on screens it wasn't meant for. Your mobile ads should be mobile only, unless Facebook automatically optimizes it for all types of screens (again, you're going to have to pay attention to your previews).

When you're selecting your ad placements, think about how far your ad is going to go. You may be tempted to select everything because of the potential reach. Don't do it. If an ad that wasn't designed for a certain screen ends up there, it will look bad and so will your business.

Mobile Marketing

Don't think of Facebook Mobile as a user-end only app. As a creator, you can use it to your benefit, and have your business in your pocket wherever you go. While it's still recommended that you have access to Facebook's desktop version (as it is more efficient in many areas), Mobile is a great way to maintain your social media marketing, especially when it comes to engagement.

Naturally, you'll have to install the app (and Messenger) onto your phone. There is a risk that you might use them to vegetate instead of work, but the only way around this is to control yourself. Other than that, there aren't many (or any) drawbacks to using Facebook Mobile alongside the desktop version. On the contrary, there are perks.

Accessing Facebook from your phone is faster and easier than logging onto the website. The app is also handy for staying on top of your personal notifications, and for using Messenger for business. There are also extra Facebook apps that will help you streamline your advertising and marketing from your phone. The list includes, but isn't limited to, three important and handy ones that I urge you to download and try for yourself.

Facebook Pages Manager is exactly what it sounds like. It has faced a few bugs in its time but it still has its place and can definitely help you keep your business page organized. The problem with Facebook mobile is that it places emphasis on personal accounts, and often hides or ignores notifications to do with pages. From the Pages Manager app, you can stay logged into your business page without switching back and forth. You can keep up to date with any messages your page has received, view and manage your insights, and of course post to your page.

Facebook Ads Manager makes it easy for entrepreneurs to manage all aspects of their ads. Using it, you can track your ad's performance, investigate your ad analytics, manage your expenses and budget, and edit and create ads. Some users say that it is glitchy, and although it works well, it's better to double check everything on your computer before you publish. Still, what a cool way to create ads on the go.

Facebook Analytics is the app for you if you're not interested in managing or creating anything from your phone, but still want to keep an eye on things. This app doesn't equip you to make any changes to your accounts, but it breaks down and organizes your analytics across all of your pages and ads. You can even have visual representations of your analytics as graphs. It's purely informational, but it's an important app to have. Did I mention that it sends you important alerts, and has insights that the other apps don't?

What You Can't Do With Your Phone

It's not recommended that you rely solely on Facebook mobile to get your marketing done. It works well as a supplement to the full desktop version, but it doesn't have as many features, is limited in its display, and overall isn't as efficient as the website.

Though you can create ads in the Ads Manager app, it may be difficult to build ads from scratch, especially if you have a smaller phone. This is especially true for creating video ads, so if ever you use any of the mobile apps to create ads do your best to have your material ready for upload without edits.

Unless you download the Analytics app, you won't be able to see all of your insights. Designing or revamping your page will be a pain too, more so if you can't check on a desktop to make sure that's nothing's out of place or misaligned. Facebook Mobile is also a bit unreliable with page notifications, so don't count on it to alert you to everything that goes on with your business.

Using your phone has cool advantages over desktop because it makes it easier to interact with your audience and check up on your work. Still, it's better to have the desktop version as your base, and the Facebook apps for when you're on the go.

The Takeaway

The only way to effectively market on Facebook is to market to the whole of Facebook. Mobile users are undeniably the majority of Facebook's population and you can't afford to leave mobile marketing out of the equation. Still, dealing with all the variables like screen sizes, operating systems, and device capacities is a struggle and there is no way that you will be able to please everyone.

You can use Facebook Mobile, and other handy Facebook apps for administration on the go. What's more important, though, is to use them for interactions, communications and engagement.

Chapter 5: The Marketplace

I'm not sure if you remember this after all the lessons you've had to take in, but Facebook has its own classifieds called the Marketplace. You might assume that there isn't much to do there, and that it's more of a Craigslist type listing that is more apt for private sellers and noticeboard style ads, but you'd be wrong. The Marketplace can boost your professional business, if you know how to use it.

Something that most entrepreneurs overlook is that the Facebook Marketplace is literally a business center, full of people willing to spend money on the deals that they find there. Think of it as the shopping mall of the platform. You may stumble upon one or two crazy characters that have glaring red flags when it comes to trust, but for the most part it's a place for people looking to do business.

When we think of the Marketplace, we imagine it as a hub for secondhand goods and unprofessional ads. Someone who is looking to get rid of their old bike wouldn't pay for the song and dance of an ad campaign, but they would list it in the classifieds and hope that someone out there will match their set price. They'll negotiate, and most likely never see or talk to their "customer" ever again after the sale is made. The Marketplace place doesn't charge you to list anything in it, nor will it take a fee. So, you can advertise anything at any price and make 100% profit.

It may not be ideal for your brand, but there's money to be made and you shouldn't disregard the Marketplace simply because it's not an official marketing tool. That said, it's a bit of a strange place. Let's take a quick walk through it so that you know what you're dealing with.

The Money Market

The Marketplace is for merchants that are selling physical products, so unfortunately if your business offers a service to customers you won't be able to promote yourself in its listings. That doesn't mean that you can't still take advantage of the Marketplace. I'll explain in a moment.

If you have a product that falls in line with the Marketplace's regulations, nothing is preventing you from listing it. It's not quite the same as having someone approach your business to buy from you, but if you're a small business a sale is a sale. There are no costs involved in showcasing your products on the Marketplace, so it's a free and effortless way of expanding your reach and pulling in new customers. This can work wonders for your brand.

But before you jump right in, there are some key things you should understand about the Marketplace. Though it's a place for merchants selling tangible objects on their own terms to whomever they select, there are a lot of regulations regarding what you can do there.

What You Can Sell

To start off, the Marketplace is still under Facebook's domain and therefore you will have to abide by all of Facebook's terms of service and community standards. So, everything I mentioned earlier, like engagement-baiting, false advertising, or misrepresentation are still no-gos.

Then, there's quite a long list of restrictions on what you can sell (Commerce Policies, n.d.). Banned products include: medicine, drugs, supplements, and related paraphernalia (including alcohol and tobacco); weapons and their components, and explosives; live animals; adult or overtly sexual products; most healthcare products; digital media and some electronics; anything considered hazardous; gambling aids, currency, or documents; body parts, bodily fluids, and anything related to human trafficking.

Beyond the regulations of what's not allowed, you can sell vehicles and also rental properties. In some cases, you can request that Facebook approve certain restricted products but there is no guarantee that your listing will be approved.

It's worth noting that these are not just the Marketplace's regulations—it's Facebook's commerce policy. If you attempt to disobey them, you could be banned from the platform entirely and lose your business and advertising accounts. It's best to play it safe and stick to the rules.

Advertising Vs Listing

Say you have a product that the Marketplace will accept. Which is better? Listing it in the Marketplace and making 100% profit, or advertising it all over Facebook for a fee? Honestly, both are good ideas and you should seriously consider using them to boost your business. Think about it, the Marketplace is free, so listing your products there won't cost you anything extra if you still choose to advertise on Facebook. What do you have to lose?

More importantly, you can place official Facebook ads in the Marketplace. This is huge, because as I said, people who are browsing the Marketplace already have high buying attention. If your ad catches their eye, it's likely that they will pay attention to it. Since you're simply placing official ads inside the Marketplace and not listing, you can promote your business even if you do offer a service.

If you're interested, here's how to do both, and a few things to keep in mind if you do.

Listing Products in Facebook Marketplace

Selling directly from the Marketplace is one of the easiest things in the world. You can list your products as an individual or as a business, so think about which one will best serve your marketing strategy. I'd recommend making the listing as your brand, because it will link your page automatically and could bring you new likes and followers.

Step 1: Navigate to Marketplace. You will find it in Facebook's main menu, on the left of your screen. It doesn't matter which account you are signed into at this stage.

Step 2: Click on "Sell Something" and then select "Item for Sale". Facebook will ask you who you want to sell as. If you'd like to list as your brand, select your account from the list before you continue.

Step 3: Input your product information. Here, you will have to name your item, list a price, set your location and pick the most accurate category. You also have the option to fill in a description of what you're selling. This is recommended if you are building brand awareness, as it's an opportunity to state the facts about your business or product.

Step 4: You can now add up to 10 photos of your product. They don't have to be professional photos, but make sure that they are clear, accurate, and eye catching.

Step 5: Hit "Post" and your listing will appear on the Marketplace.

How to Place Ads in the Marketplace

To set up an official ad in the Marketplace navigate to your Ads Manager and create or edit an ad as instructed earlier. Once you have defined your objective and audience, you will have an option to define your ad's placement. You can choose between "Automatic Placement" or "Edit Placement".

If you choose Automatic Placement, Facebook will list your ad wherever it's suitable, including the Marketplace, so this is the recommended option. There isn't any way to set your ads to appear in the Marketplace only. If you choose "Edit Placement" and select Marketplace, your ad will appear in the News Feed as well by default.

Once you have made your selection, you will continue setting up your ad as previously described, choosing your format or medium, budget, and schedule.

Listing Beyond the Marketplace

In case you didn't know, the Marketplace and Collection or Carousel ads aren't the only ways that you can list your products on Facebook. You can run an online store from your business page, using

Facebook's built in 'Store' tab on your business page.

You have two choices when setting up your Facebook store: you can list and sell directly from Facebook, using the website's integrated checkout and payment system, or you can set up an ecommerce site (like Shopify) on an external platform and link it to your Facebook store page.

Either way is efficient, though the consensus is that selling directly from Facebook, though simpler at first, is the more limited of the two. A few issues you might run into are fewer payment options for customers and some features that are U.S. only. Another problem is that if you use Facebook directly you can only sell tangible items through your store.

On the other hand, if you build your own ecommerce store outside of the website your products will still be accessible to people who don't use Facebook, so you'll have more reach. You'll be able to customize your own platform and won't be restricted by Facebook's features. If you're offering a service or digital product you will still be able to list them.

Though linking a third-party store to Facebook's store seems like it has more perks, there will be a learning curve and depending on the host you choose, it may cost you a subscription fee. If you're building your store on a fully customizable platform like Wix or WordPress, you'll have to design your store from scratch and consider domain and hosting fees too.

Regardless of the road you take, I just want to emphasize that if you aren't comfortable listing products in the Marketplace, there are similar options on Facebook, even if you are not using it directly.

Navigating the Marketplace

Fascinating as the Marketplace may be, it's not for everyone and may not suit your business well. There are some risks involved with marketing there, and you must understand that it works slightly differently to how business pages, or even your personal profile does.

The biggest difference between Facebook's main platform and its Marketplace is clear. One is a spot for people to connect with friends, followers, and supporters; the other is a classified solely for the buying and selling of goods. Don't expect the Marketplace to be anything like your main account or business page. Though there is nothing wrong with using the Marketplace, it can be said that it is less sophisticated than other corners of Facebook.

You have to keep in mind that you will be communicating with perfect strangers who may not necessarily like you or your brand and just want your product for the cheapest price possible. Most people in the Marketplace will attempt to negotiate your prices, so you must prepare to stand your ground if your price isn't up for discussion. You'd be surprised at how many people will try their luck, even if you clearly state that your price is fixed.

Unlike Facebook's store (or any other e-store for that matter) payments are your responsibility and will have to be handled one on one with your customer. You will have to be diligent with this, because there is ample opportunity for swindling.

Speaking of which, the people you sell to may not be honest about who they are. There are safety risks involved in giving away your information, so be careful with your delivery of your products, and how many personal details you share.

When it comes to your business, there are also one or two considerations. Since people browsing the Marketplace are mostly searching for bargains, you may come across unpleasant characters who, if they don't get their way, could take issue with your entire brand and leave unfair negative reviews on your page. Although the Marketplace is as good a platform as any, there is still an unprofessional stigma attached to it. If you frequent it, or only get business through it, you run the risk of not being taken seriously outside of it.

Speaking of which, is the Marketplace appropriate for serious entrepreneurs? Of course, it is. If you handle your affairs there with tact and professionalism, you can make a lot of money by going to potential customers instead of waiting for them to come to you. It's an opportunity, like any other. Wise entrepreneurs will try it out, even if they choose not to commit to it in the end.

The Takeaway

Facebook's Marketplace is an underrated way to sell your products and build brand awareness if you aren't too shy to put yourself out there. It may not be the most sophisticated way to make money or market yourself on the platform, but it is a smart consideration if you're looking to sell your products quickly and easily.

Before you list in the Marketplace, you must understand that it does not have the same backing as an ecommerce store. You will have to handle your transactions and rapport all on your own, and there are ways that you could be scammed, catfished, or otherwise tricked by your customers.

If you don't want your products listed in the Marketplace, or if you are selling a service instead, you can still place ads inside it. The Marketplace is where eager spenders are, so it would be a mistake to disregard it.

Chapter 6: Facebook Jail

Advertising and marketing on Facebook are all fun and games until things go wrong. Facebook isn't a perfect platform, so unfortunately, it's inevitable that you will face some issues when you promote yourself there.

Because Facebook is such a large platform, potential problems cover a wide spectrum, from technical problems with your ads to restrictions placed on your account, to the scores of controversies and criticisms that both the website and its founder have received and the impact of such on the users.

It's nothing you can't handle, but I'd like to make you aware of some of these troubles to make your marketing venture as painless as possible.

Common Complaints

There are millions of businesses currently advertising on Facebook, and that means that there are millions of potential problems when it comes to advertising. It would be impossible to list every single issue there is, so let's stick to the most typical ones. The three most common complaints among Facebook marketers and advertisers are:

- **Your ad has been rejected or removed:** Facebook has cracked down on the content that is shared on the platform and ads are no exception. There is always a risk that your ad will be removed even if Facebook approves it because of something that you can't control: the customers. Facebook users are becoming a little bit too comfortable with the report button, and because Facebook's regulation (or censorship in some cases) has become so strict, you could see your ad reviewed, pulled, or even banned. Unfortunately, there isn't any way around this if it is the viewer's doing. The most you can do is stick to Facebook's community standards and hope for the best. If, at any point, your ad gets into trouble you will have the option to appeal and restore it, but this will be at the sole discretion of Facebook moderators. Your best bet is to play by the rules. Most of the time if your ad is rejected or removed, you will get a clue as to why. If your content goes against Facebook's rules, your only choice will be to start again and change what got you reported or rejected in the first place.

- **Your ad's quality has deteriorated, or your ad doesn't look right:** This is likely a formatting issue. If you upload sub-quality promotional content, Facebook's engine may deteriorate it even further. Your only solution is prevention. Make sure that you have created your ad within Facebook's recommended specs so that in the event of quality loss, it won't be as crushing or as noticeable. If, on the other hand, you uploaded perfectly formatted and sized content but it looks like garbage after it's been published, the only thing you can do is report the technical problem to Facebook from the post itself. Currently, this only applies to video playback, but you can always reach out to Facebook's help center to manually explain the issue you are experiencing.

- **Your ad is not performing well:** This isn't a true troubleshooting problem, but it's still worth a mention. Your ad may not be driving conversions as well as you hoped it would for a number of reasons, including insufficient market research, shoddy design, timing and scheduling, and relevance. These are all things you will have to evaluate and analyze to correct. The best way to keep tabs on your ads performance is to check your analytics and user feedback, and also to run split tests to see what flies and what bombs. A split test is when you run different versions of the same ad to determine which elements work best for it. It could be changes in your copy, color scheme, imagery, CTA, or other factors. If you are ever undecided in which ad campaign to commit to, split tests aren't an option, they're necessary. They're also a great way to see what captivates your audience and will give you insight into what needs more attention and what you can do without in your marketing.

Keep in mind that for almost all problems on Facebook, in marketing or otherwise, you can check Facebook's help guides. If you don't find what you're looking for, you can contact the Facebook team for further assistance.

Terms and Conditions Apply

When you sign up for Facebook, you are agreeing to play by its rules. This isn't always a good thing. Facebook is certainly one of the nicer hangouts online, but it's not without fault and scandal. In fact, 2018 alone was enough for Facebook to get into trouble at least 21 times. The drama ranged from the previously mentioned Facebook-Cambridge Analytica Data Scandal, to accusations that Facebook fueled genocidal fires, to discussion of the platform's political alignment and bias. It was a crazy year for the website and its employees (Issie Lapowsky, 2018).

The effects of such can still be felt in 2020, with constant talks of Facebook's 'spying', discrimination in censorship, lax security leading to many hack attacks, and unjustified distribution of user data. In fact, as recently as January 2020 the company felt significant drops in stock value and annual profit, hitting its lowest point since 2014 (Matyus, 2020).

In an effort to restore both its reputation and its good standing, users are noticing new regulations that are meant to protect all concerned, but in reality dampen the experience of using the platform, especially if Facebook is vital to your business.

One example of this is Facebook's regulation on "Issues Ads". This came into play not long after the Facebook-Cambridge Analytica scandal, and is likely an attempt to clean up some of the mess it made. Issues ads are defined as any ad that promotes a political or societal problem, standing, or opinion. It's not that such ads are totally banned from the platform, but that they're screened before they're published, and require more transparency than ordinary business ads. Topics include, but aren't limited to, guns and weaponry, abortion, politics, civil rights, environmental issues, crime, education, poverty and even health (Hutchinson, 2018). Even if you think that this doesn't affect you because your products have nothing to do with these topics, these are mostly umbrella keywords and it's nearly impossible to say what counts as issues and what doesn't. Furthermore, if your brand takes a stand on something that is important to you—or if you run a campaign for donations and support for a cause—Facebook might put you in the dog box. It's unlikely, but not impossible or unheard of.

This introduces the concept of "Facebook Jail"—a mild inconvenience to ordinary users, and a massive problem to entrepreneurs. If Facebook detects that the content you are posting, sharing, or marketing goes against its community standards, your entire account could be suspended or permanently removed from the platform. While it's great that Facebook makes an effort to keep the website a safe space for all, many people believe that its regulation is too strict and is borderline totalitarian.

Generally speaking, any content that violates community standards could get you banned; topics that often violate standards include violence, sexual content, hate speech and insensitivity, or cruelty. The problem is that these topics are not clearly defined and Facebook's machines are not good at discerning innocence from attacks. One example of this, was the controversial "Men Are Trash" discussion.

With the rise of domestic and sexual violence against women, social media users spread this particular hashtag to emphasize toxic masculinity's effects on the world. Facebook deemed it hate speech and the mere mention of the hashtag, whether in support or criticism, became a violation (Newton, 2019).

It might not look like this affects business, but instances like the aforementioned censorship could break you. If you post, share, or support content that Facebook doesn't approve of from your personal profile, you stand to be locked out of your account. If you are, you won't be able to access any of your connected accounts, which means you won't be able to manage your business. Some users also experience shadow bans—wherein their content and accounts are still active, but made invisible to everyone else. Naturally this negates the entire concept of engagement and networking and could cause your entire business to plummet.

The Takeaway

Facebook is a fantastic platform for businesses but thanks to its own mistakes, crimes, and misdemeanors the website has changed to be stricter, tighter, and more controlled. This not only affects casual users, it affects businesses and advertisers too, perhaps even more so than the former.

If you get kicked off of Facebook, you won't be able to recover your business that is set up on it. You have to be very careful in what you say, share, and promote to prevent this. While you can't control what others don't like and report, if you conduct yourself according to Facebook's community standards, you'll at least have a chance to appeal their suspensions or bans.

On a lighter note, most technical issues in marketing are easily solved. One of the perks of Facebook's size is that its tech support is easy to get a hold of and have a good track record of managing user communications. Most technical issues can also be prevented by playing by the rules and taking extra steps to test your ads before you run them.

Chapter 7: Rethinking Your Brand

We've taken an in-depth look at Facebook's platform, so you should have a solid understanding of what you've done wrong or misunderstood in the past. If anything, the takeaway from this book should be that Facebook is not a miracle machine that you can sign up to and instantly become a tycoon. It's a complex social network that has its own modus operandi—one that will work to your advantage if you understand and cooperate with it or work to your detriment if you disregard it.

Regardless of how you advertise on Facebook there's one thing that all businesses have to make a priority: your brand. All the advertising in the world won't help you if your brand isn't taken seriously, or if you are sorely unprofessional online.

So, to end off, I'd like to give you one final assignment. Using the knowledge you now have of Facebook's engine, I want you to go back and revamp your business and brand according to what you've learned. You don't have to redesign your logo or become someone you're not, but you do have to think about how you've been presenting yourself on the website.

Stay Relevant

We all have that ol' reliable brand, company, product, or idol that we love because they stayed the same. Humans are comfortable in the familiar, so it's no surprise that we often resist change. We see this frequently when it comes to entertainment. If a movie studio dares recast our favorite character, or if a musician changes their sound and style, we'll be personally offended and put off what they do. But there's a difference between selling out and adapting. Your brand has to stay relevant to retain its engagement. Don't stagnate, don't make yourself obsolete, and don't allow yourself to fall into the background. As an elementary marketer it may have been okay to post infrequently or only when you felt it was important. However, social media functions on trends—trends that are quickly forgotten and replaced. You may experience a boom in attention because you correlate to what's trending, but when the hype dies down, so will your business.

Don't ever spam your audience with the same stale content over and over again, but do make an effort to stay visible. Marketing isn't always advertising. Your commentary on a hot topic, stories of your embarrassing blunders or brain farts, records of your wins and successes, or even bonus content like vlogs, blogs, or hangouts in live streams could keep you front and center. At the end of the day, humans are most likely to give attention to accounts that are authentic. Show your humanity every now and then and people will remember that you're not a robot, and that you can post silly and fun things in between your talks of business. It will also keep you relevant. If all you do is advertise, you'll only come to mind when it's necessary. If you post frequently, whether you're discussing business or not, you're more likely to spread on word of mouth. This could lead to recommendations, and in turn conversions.

Optimize Your Business Page

Admit it. Your Facebook business page needs some work. No one gets it right the first time and elementary marketers, especially those without experience, tend to try a little too hard to be captivating. That, or your page may be somewhat underwhelming because you told yourself that you'd "return to it later". Did you? Don't lie to me, I know you didn't. Think of your Facebook page as the exterior of a brick and mortar shop. If there are bullet holes in the windows, its and paint is peeling, and someone graffitied curse words all over your door then customers aren't likely to enter. First impressions count for everything in business, and if a new person takes a look at your page and isn't compelled to stay, you'll probably never see them again. so here's what I want you to do:

- **Customize your URL and Handle:** Searching for your business shouldn't be difficult to do, but often company names are similar and it amounts to confusion. Why tell someone to check out your Facebook page if you're going to follow up with "it's the account with the blue and yellow logo and stars in the background, but not the one with the dog, the one with the smiley face and the cityscape", when you can simply tell them to visit "Facebook dot com slash your Facebook page". You can customize your page's URL (but choose wisely, in most cases you only get one chance). You can also customize your page's handle to make it easier to search and tag. A word of advice, if your brand's name is Placeholder Page, your URL and your handle should reflect it, exactly if possible.

- **Fill out Your Information, Properly This Time:** The About section on your page is crucial for business. This may be a matter of opinion, but there are few things as frustrating to me as taking a look at a page (say, if friends have invited me to like it) and having no idea of what it's for. If you sell shoes, let your customers know that. Please, I am begging you, don't just put the year you founded your brand and "please support me" in your description. It's one of the fastest ways to deter potential customers. Tell me that you sell shoes. Tell me if they're handcrafted, or important, or vegan-friendly. Do you sell shoes to men with gigantic feet, or only to teen girls looking to add some sparkle to their prom dresses and pageant outfits? The trick is to show people that you can fulfil their needs. Try to have a little bit of personality without cluttering your About section with unnecessary information. While it's lovely that your grandmother taught you how to sew and now you're capitalizing on your inherited skill, no one cares that your Grandmother went to private school and got married when she was 19, or that you fell on your head as a baby, or that you're allergic to peanuts. Remember your about section is for your brand, not you. It's cool to say that your office is full of cats. It's excessive to point out that cats are your favorite animal. See? Beyond your About section, you'll also want to keep your contact information, location, personnel, and affiliates or partnerships up to date. You also have the option to upload a featured video, so if you have a good promo don't forget to showcase it. Update your gallery while you're at it, and fix any formatting errors with your profile or cover pictures.

- **Branch Out:** Make use of Facebook's features. Most beginner marketers start with the obvious: updating their statuses, sharing photos and videos, and paying for ads. I've already covered the marketplace, but there other avenues I bet you haven't gone down. Use SEO and hashtags when you post, update your stories, start a group, livestream, set up polls, and make sure that your business page has an engaging autoresponder in Messenger. Don't forget to tap into your insights and analytics to see how your page and posts are doing. Facebook is so much more than just posting what's on your mind, so don't limit yourself to its basic functions.

- **Declutter:** There's no harm in tidying up your page and it's recommended that you do, especially if your first attempt at marketing was full of the no-gos, like engagement-baiting, or spam. Again, you can use your analytics and insights to gauge which posts were barely seen, and you're fully within your rights to remove them. The same applies to unflattering or low quality photos and videos. You don't have to atom bomb your page, and you must not look like you're covering something up, but a little spring cleaning can make your page more sophisticated and therefore, more engaging.

How to be a Better Marketer

Ultimately, it doesn't matter if you put everything I have mentioned into practice perfectly if you don't understand what marketing is. It's the action of promoting a brand, business, product, or service with the hope that there will be monetary gain after all is said and done. It goes a lot further than simply posting links to your webstore and saying, "buy my stuff, thanks". Marketing takes a fair amount of skill, and there are some essentials you can't do without, even if it means that the only way to up your Facebook game is to hire a content manager to do it for you.

Now that you understand how Facebook works, here's what's expected from you as an intermediate Facebook Marketer:

- Strong communication, be it written, spoken, or visual. In a perfect world, it would be all three.
- An understanding of strategy. You need this to be able to plan ahead.
- Rapport, not just in your communication but in your management of it. Reply to your messages, acknowledge your comments, answer customer queries, and stay on top of your criticism, discrepancies or customer complaints.

- Work ethic is important too. Marketing won't matter if you only do it once every six months and never follow through.
- Creativity. It can't really be taught, but the last thing you want is to bore people. You must understand, and be able to fulfil, customer interest. Run of the mill posts simply won't drive engagement.
- Up-to-date resources are necessary. Technology is constantly advancing. If you're still using a computer from 2003, you're not getting the full Facebook or marketing experience. Updating your tools and services is vital to stay in the game.
- You have to think like a business person. Remember that you're not trying to get attention, you're trying to make money. Reach is a means to an end, not the goal.

These are all skills that anyone can learn if they put enough time and effort into it. Don't be afraid to read further, take a course, or even learn through experience. It's cliché, but Rome wasn't built in a day, and your empire won't be either. Marketing on Facebook will speed up your journey to domination, but the most important trait you need as an intermediate Facebook marketer is patience. Facebook isn't going anywhere, so don't rush it, don't force it, and don't forget to enjoy yourself.

Most people use Facebook for fun. You may be a professional, but you're no exception.

Conclusion: Beyond Facebook

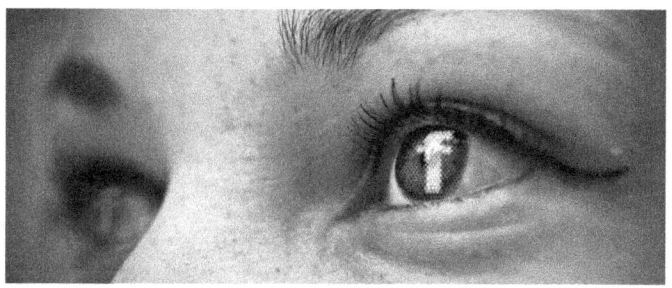

It may not be perceived as the trendiest place to be, but the numbers don't lie. Businesses can't afford to overlook or disregard the power of Facebook marketing. You've got that down, and well done for digging deeper into Facebook's advertising prowess. But the most important thing to remember is that the power doesn't lie in using Facebook; it lies in making Facebook work for you.

As a marketer, you may be wondering where you can go once you've nailed your Facebook marketing. It would be silly to assume that you rely solely on Facebook for reach, sales, or engagement because there are countless other online tools and platforms that you can (and should) use to grow your business.

Signing up for these services is a fantastic idea, but what you have to remember is that the way it is right now, and the way it's looking for the future, Facebook is the most important social media (and therefore, marketing) tool at your disposal.

So, where to from here? Honestly, nowhere. In emphasizing Facebook marketing, you are exactly where you need to be as a business. There is no beyond, at least not for now (and probably not for a long time). Facebook is here to stay. It's where the grass is greenest, if you know what I mean.

References

Altmann, G. (2016). Facebook Internet Network Social. In Pixabay. https://pixabay.com/photos/Facebook-internet-network-social-1903445/

Andersen, D. (2019, October 5). 20 Facebook Advertising Statistics You Need to Know in 2020. DialogTech. https://www.dialogtech.com/blog/Facebook-statistics/

Andrews, M. (2017, February 16). Supercharge Your Content With Shutterstock for HubSpot. Blog.Hubspot.Com. https://blog.hubspot.com/customers/shutterstock-hubspot-integration-partnership

Boyd, J. (2019). The Facebook Algorithm Explained and How to Work it. Brandwatch. https://www.brandwatch.com/blog/the-Facebook-algorithm-explained/

Cakebread, C. (2017, November 15). You're not alone, no one reads terms of service agreements. Business Insider.

https://www.businessinsider.com/deloitte-study-91-percent-agree-terms-of-service-without-reading-2017-11?IR=T

Commerce Policies. (n.d.). Www.Facebook.Com. Retrieved February 19, 2020, from https://www.Facebook.com/policies/commerce

Community Standards | Facebook. (n.d.). Www.Facebook.Com. Retrieved February 17, 2020, from https://www.Facebook.com/communitystandards/misrepresentation/

Daffodil Software. (2017, July 31). 9 Applications of Machine Learning from Day-to-Day Life. Medium; App Affairs. https://medium.com/app-affairs/9-applications-of-machine-learning-from-day-to-day-life-112a47a429d0

Donie O'Sullivan, CNN Business. (2019, March 14). It took Facebook 15 years to take over the world. Here's how. CNN. https://edition.cnn.com/2019/03/14/tech/Facebook-outage-resolved/index.html

Dopson, E. (2019, March 13). Videos vs. Images: Which Drives More Engagement in Facebook Ads? | Databox Blog. Databox. https://databox.com/videos-vs-images-in-Facebook-ads

Ekine, R. (2017). Visual content trends that dominate Facebook. Newsfeed.Org. https://newsfeed.org/visual-content-trends-that-dominate-Facebook/

Enrico, R. (n.d.). What Marketers Need to Know About Facebook Carousel Ads. Convince and Convert: Social Media Consulting and Content Marketing Consulting. Retrieved February 18, 2020, from https://www.convinceandconvert.com/social-media-strategy/Facebook-carousel-ads/

Facebook Image Ad Specs for Facebook Feed, Reach ad objective. (2019). Facebook Ads Guide. https://www.Facebook.com/business/ads-guide/image

Horsman, G. (2016, May 31). What Ever Happened To Friendster? - A Lesson Learned. Website Design | Internet Marketing | WordPress Websites. https://www.aglobalreach.com/what-happened-to-friendster/

Hutchinson, A. (2018, May 9). Facebook Releases List of "Issues Ads" Which Will Require Increased Transparency. Social Media Today. https://www.socialmediatoday.com/news/Facebook-releases-list-of-issues-ads-which-will-require-increased-transpa/523120/

Issie Lapowsky. (2018, December 20). The 21 (and Counting) Biggest Facebook Scandals of 2018. Wired; WIRED. https://www.wired.com/story/Facebook-scandals-2018/

Iven, W. (n.d.). Social Media Facebook Smartphone. Retrieved May 14, 2015, from https://pixabay.com/photos/social-media-Facebook-smartphone-763731/

Learn About Lookalike Audiences | Facebook Ads Help Center. (2019). Facebook Ads Help Center. https://www.Facebook.com/business/help/164749007013531?id=401668390442328

Lee, A. (2011, June 30). Myspace Collapse: How The Social Network Fell Apart. HuffPost Canada; HuffPost Canada. https://www.huffpost.com/entry/how-myspace-fell-apart_n_887853

Linforth, P. (2015). Facebook Icon Like. In Pixabay. https://pixabay.com/illustrations/Facebook-icon-like-thumb-1084449/

Matyus, A. (2020, January 30). After years of scandals, Facebook is finally starting to feel the fallout. Digital Trends; Digital Trends. https://www.digitaltrends.com/news/after-years-of-scandals-Facebook-is-finally-starting-to-feel-the-fallout/

Morey, R. (2018, January 29). The 5 Types of Engagement Bait Facebook Is Fighting. Revive Social. https://revive.social/Facebook-engagement-bait/

Mosseri, A. (2018, January 12). Bringing People Closer Together. About Facebook. https://about.fb.com/news/2018/01/news-feed-fyi-bringing-people-closer-together/

Newton, C. (2019, October 3). Why you can't say 'men are trash' on Facebook. The Verge. https://www.theverge.com/interface/2019/10/3/20895119/Facebook-men-are-trash-hate-speech-zuckerberg-leaked-audio

Perry, A. (2019, December 16). Facebook owns the 4 most downloaded apps of the decade. Mashable. https://mashable.com/article/Facebook-most-downloaded-apps-2010s/

Phillips, S. (2017, July 15). A brief history of Facebook. The Guardian; The Guardian. https://www.theguardian.com/technology/2007/jul/25/media.newmedia

Rothkopf, E. (2014, May 3). Photography-Based Advertising in the Digital Age: A New System of

Meaning-Making | CCTP-725: Remix and Dialogic Culture. Georgetown.Edu. https://blogs.commons.georgetown.edu/cctp-725-fall2014/2014/05/02/photography-based-advertising-in-the-digital-age-a-new-system-of-meaning-making/

Salman Aslam. (2019, January 6). • Facebook by the Numbers (2019): Stats, Demographics & Fun Facts. Omnicoreagency.Com. https://www.omnicoreagency.com/Facebook-statistics/

Sam Biddle. (2018, April 13). Facebook Uses Artificial Intelligence to Predict Your Future Actions for Advertisers, Says Confidential Document. The Intercept. https://theintercept.com/2018/04/13/Facebook-advertising-data-artificial-intelligence-ai/

Siddigui Jr, O. (2010, May 14). History of Print Advertising. EzineArticles. https://ezinearticles.com/?History-of-Print-Advertising&id=4293897

Smith, A. (2019). Cup of coffee on laptop. In Unsplash. https://unsplash.com/photos/vuWCq1bXZy0

Specifications for Facebook Pixel Standard Events. (n.d.). Facebook Business Help Center. Retrieved

February 16, 2020, from https://www.Facebook.com/business/help/402791146561655?id=1205376682832142

Steinberger, S. (2013). Social Network Facebook. https://pixabay.com/illustrations/social-network-Facebook-network-76532/

Stout, D. (2019, July 8). Social Media Statistics: Top Social Networks by Popularity. Dustin Stout. https://dustinstout.com/social-media-statistics/

Succo. (2015). Keyboard Sure Privacy Policy. In Pixabay. https://pixabay.com/photos/keyboard-sure-privacy-policy-castle-628703/

Taylor, A. (2007, July 19). Mad Men (No. 1). AMC.

Tulie Finley-Moise. (2019, June 30). Why is Everyone Updating Their Privacy Policy (and What to Look For)? Hp.Com; HP. https://store.hp.com/us/en/tech-takes/updating-privacy-policy

Vrountas, T. (2016, July 8). The Facebook 20% Rule: Why Your Ads Might Not Be Running. Instapage.Com. https://instapage.com/blog/Facebook-20-text-rule

Zakowski, A. (2015, October 7). The Advanced Guide to Facebook Video Ads. Aaron Zakowski - Facebook Ads for SaaS Startups. https://aaronzakowski.com/guide-Facebook-video-ads/

www.ingramcontent.com/pod-product-compliance
Lightning Source LLC
Chambersburg PA
CBHW052359220526
45465CB00003BB/1176